MASTERING AND BUILDING THROUGH WORDS.

THE ART OF AFFECTING ONE'S DESTINY.

Jean Paul Tshibangu

Translated by Christelle Akiewa

BOW Media, Atlanta, 2024

Copyright © 2024 **Jean Paul Tshibangu**

MASTERING AND BUILDING THROUGH WORDS.

THE ART OF AFFECTING ONE'S DESTINY.

All Rights Reserved.

This book or any portion thereof may not be reproduced or used in any manner whatsoever without the express written permission of the publisher except for the use of brief quotations in the book review.

BOW Media, Atlanta, 2024

Printed in United States of America.
For more information, or to book an event, contact:
http://www.bowmovement.org

CONTENTS

DEDICATION 4

ACKNOWLEDGEMENT 5

ACRONYMS.. 6

PREFACE 7

INTRODUCTION 9

CHAPTER 1 - THE WORD BEFORE ANY BEGINNING 13

CHAPTER 2 - THE POWER OF THE NAME AS WORD/ THE NAMING PROCESS 31

CHAPTER 3 - COMMAND BY THE WORD 57

CHAPTER 4 - EVERYTHING RESPONDS TO THE WORD 67

CHAPTER 5 - MAKING THINGS THAT ARE INVISIBLE VISIBLE... 75

CHAPITER 6 - PRAYER AS ADVOCACY 81

CHAPTER 7 - SPEAKING IN TONGUES TO BUILD AND STRENGTHEN YOUR DESTINY 121

CHAPTER 8 - THE WORDS THAT IMPACT YOUR DESTINY AND THAT OF YOUR OFFSPRING 145

CONCLUSION.. 165

DEDICATION

I dedicate this book to the memory of my dear mother Françoise Nseya Tshibangu who passed away on April 19, 2021. Her words and prayers were the basis not only for my physical birth but also for my spirituel rebirth. I am especially grateful for her spiritual legacy.

ACKNOWLEDGEMENTS

I am very grateful to God for this inspiration and revelation that resulted in this book, the continuation of the first one on the Words, the creation and production technology. The finished work was only possible with the help and support of all these personalities who deserve my gratitude. They have allowed the correction, the comments and the improvement of the content as well as the form of this work. Please accept my gratitude and may the Almighty God bless you. I would like to mention Dr. Jean Claude Ntumba, Professor Guekaya, Pastor Jean Pierre Kazongo, Pastor Jean Jacques Sinyembo, Bibiche Sinyembo, Ange Tshibangu, Jason Amla of WithJas.

Special thanks to Christelle Akiewa who translated this book and the spirit of its revelation from French into English

ACRONYMS

AMP: Amplified Bible
ASV: American Standard Version
ESV: English Standard Version
NIV: New International Version
KJV: King James Version
CEB: Common English Bible
CEV: Contemporary English Version
EASY: Easy English Bible

Unless otherwise indicated, all Scripture quotations are taken from the English Standard Version.

PREFACE

I have personally known Reverend Pastor Jean Paul Tshibangu in various capacities for over 25 years. He is a passionate servant of God, an evangelist, and a shepherd.

By God's grace, I have discovered him as a writer, and I am happy because it is time for the knowledge, wisdom, and power of God, to which we are exposed in each of his preachings and interventions, to be made accessible to the entire body of Christ, especially, and to the world in general!

In this work, "Mastering & Building by Words," Pastor Jean Paul demonstrates to us that it is time for the body of Christ, parents, and everyone, at their level, to understand that a closed mouth is a closed destiny!

The Pastor teaches us principles such as there is no beginning without the word, the power of naming, declaration precedes possession, etc., and he firmly establishes powerful truths in our minds so that we can master and build by words.

I wish Pastor Jean Paul great success in his writing career, and through this work, may lives be transformed, destinies be opened, and captives be freed from all forms of prisons, especially that of ignorance, in the Name of Our Lord Jesus Christ.

Enjoy diving into the depths of revelation!

Pastor Jean Jacques Sinyembo

Founder and Senior Pastor of Rock of Ages Faith and Prayer Center.

INTRODUCTION

This second volume continues the reflection and study on "The words, the technology of creation and production", obviously with an emphasis on strategic words and prayers. After laying the foundations and emphasizing the importance of this technology to create, pro- duce, change and initiate things, this second part will go even deeper to extend the scope of words and their impact in many other areas.

When the architect of the Universe initiates his master-piece as told by Moses in the book of Genesis and by the Apostle John in his Gospel, it is remarkable that existence, movement, and change are only visible after the declarations, proclamations and words spoken by the Creator. The words were therefore not only the reflection of God's vision but also the trigger for their realization and materialization in the visible world.

This episode highlights the question of how to start things in the field of creation and production. What process is envisaged to ensure that the words produce and create in the best way?

Every creation and production of God in the book of the beginning was sanctioned by a name.

"God called the light Day, and the darkness he called Night. And there was evening and there was morning, the first day." **Genesis 1: 5**

Is it a coincidence that God is signing every work with a name? Wasn't naming part of the creation process? It is important to understand the importance given to this process in the spiritual world, especially since the name is a spoken word and as such deserves much attention in the spiritual world.

After creation, man also received instructions from God to rule over the different jurisdictions of the earth, waters, and heavens as developed in Volume 1.

"And God blessed them [granting them certain authority] and said to them, "Be fruitful, multiply, and fill the earth, and subjugate it [putting it under your power]; and rule over (dominate) the fish of the sea, the birds of the air, and every living thing that moves upon the earth." **Genesis 1 : 28 AMP**

The real question remains how to do it? Is not the word the means par excellence to exercise this authority over these spheres, to which he can only have access through words and prayers? One cannot dominate without commanding, without giving orders, and to this, there are always answers because everything responds to the word.

There are things that exist in the invisible, and for some of these things, it is possible to transport them into the physical world. Words and prayers are the means par excellence to bring them into the physical world. How to get there? This study will still provide the gateways to do so.

Words (prayers) can convince God to change his judgments or those invoked against us by the world of darkness. It is God himself who exhorts us to plead like Moses, the Syro-phoenician woman, Abraham, Hezekiah. For what reasons and with what arguments should we present ourselves before him? How to do it?

Words also build our destinies. It is thus relevant to understand how to use them to do this, even better, which types of words do it in the best way. Words in tongues also play a role in this construction. Awareness of this dimension allows you to better build your destiny and that of your offspring as well.

This second volume not only completes the first, but it also deepens several other concepts, revelations, and themes already discussed. It also answers the questions raised above to draw your attention to the strength, power, authority, and impact of words and prayers in any form.

CHAPTER 1

THE WORD BEFORE ANY BEGINNING

"In the beginning (before all times) was the Word (Christ) and the Word was with God, and the Word was God Himself. He was (continually existing) in the beginning (co-eternally) with God. All things were made and came into existence through Him; and without Him not even one thing was made that has come into being. In Him was life (and the power to bestow life) and the life was the Light of men." **John 1: 1 - 4 AMP.**

"In the beginning God (Elohim) created (by forming from nothing) the heavens and the earth. The earth was formless and void or a waste and emptiness, and darkness was upon the face of deep (primeval) ocean that covered the unformed earth.) The spirit of God was moving (hovering, brooding) over the face of the waters. Ang God said, "let there be light"; and there was light." **Genesis 1: 1 - 3 AMP**

It is clear from the above passages that the work of creation and the beginning was not only a matter of Jesus- Christ, but it is also the work where His divine power was manifested. There is a relationship, a connection between the Word and the creation or the beginning of everything.

There is no creation and beginning without the Word. It is God's way of doing things.

When God wants to create and to produce, He speaks, He releases the word, or He makes declarations and proclamations.

God begins everything with a Word.

Whenever God wants to start something, He begins by speaking first, that is really His way of doing things. There is nothing that God has started without first being able to speak by using a declaration, a proclamation, a command, an order, a promise or even a sentence.

The word is one of God's great activities, first at creation and then in time. Everything that God has done is a matter of the word.

The word is the "material" with which God made everything in the universe.

Nothing exists without the word.

Every situation that exists is the result as well as the consequence of the word. Therefore, every change should also be the result of a word. Nothing that is has been without a word being spoken, declared, and proclaimed.

No change without a word being spoken.

There is nothing that exists without the word. Even the devil needs a negative word or a curse to act. So, there is nothing that can change without a word being spoken or released into the atmosphere.

The word creates a situation unless another word is spoken to cancel the current effects.

Also, God does nothing without revealing His intentions and secrets to His servants the prophets (**Amos 3: 7**[1]), in other words God does nothing without speaking.

We can therefore state that:
1. When God wants to do something, He speaks, He releases a word.
2. When God wants to do something for man, He wants him to speak.
3. When God desires to intervene in people's lives, He wants speakers (intercessors).
4. When God wants to prevent something from happening, He looks for men to speak.
5. Prayer is a way for man to speak.
6. God waits for man to speak before the angels

---

1. **Amos 3: 7** *"For the Lord God does nothing without revealing his secret to his servants the prophets."*

move. The order of the angels' mission can also depend on your prayer.

7. God is waiting for us to speak so that there can be movement in heaven!
8. The word is the basis of all creation, change, transformation, or metamorphosis...

The word, level of beginning and finishing at the same time.

We must also understand God's way of working and functioning. He does not proceed as man does. He designs things in His mind. He has an idea, a thought, a vision and as a result, He will speak a word to call this thought or vision into existence so that it appears. The things that God wants to see appear, He declared, announced, and proclaimed them.

To speak in a human way and with a human language, in the phase of creation or initiation of things, the word is the most important stage of this process. It is the finishing level.

When God speaks, He is both in the beginning and in the completion of things, so when we hear God speak about an area, He has already completed that thing.

It is difficult to comprehend this if we think like man.

However, in God, time is not linear as in man, thus giving the ability to evaluate things as by a beginning and by an end.

Therefore, God is the beginning and the end because the two are not separated. God is outside of time; with Him, all things are as if in one point.

I believe that when we speak, we are at the end of what we create, begin, or call into existence.

With God, when you speak, the thing is already done. The manifestation in the visible is only a revelation of what already exists in the spiritual world.

In God the, thought (conception or decision), the word, the accomplishment, and the visibility, are as if in one point while in man, things are as if on a timeline with a moment of thought, a moment of word, a moment of fulfillment, and finally, a moment of the visibility of things.

With God, the word is the expression of the decision. Thus, the things that exist are the consequences of all that God has resolved.

When God speaks, it signifies that decisions have been made and actions have been completed. God desires for us to function in the same way. As the prophet Jeremiah poignantly states in **Lamentations 3: 37 - 38 AMP**.

"Who is there who speaks, and it comes to pass, Unless the Lord has authorized and command it? Is it from the mouth of the Most High that both adversity (misfortune) and good (prosperity, happiness) proceed?"

Through His word alone, God not only brings events to pass but also calls things into existence in the world. He is the one who decides things and expresses his resolutions in words that underlie all things, and the basis of everything. Like God, when we speak it should be the moment when things have already been decided and finished. That is why Jesus Christ invoked this principle and taught in **Mark 11: 23 AMP** that *"I assure you and most solemnly say to you, whoever says to this mountain, Be lifted up and thrown into sea! And does not doubt in his heart (in God's unlimited power) but believes that he says is going to take place, it will be done for him (in accordance with God's will)."*

It is when we say things that they happen in the spiritual world, and it is not when we see things that they are actually done or achieved. If we are to recapitulate, in the human chronology, there are these four stages which are on a timeline and placed successively as points:

1. Reflection (decision)
2. The word
3. Fulfillment
4. Visibility of things or their manifestation

It is therefore clear that things are made, realized, or accomplished in the spiritual world before they are seen, which is why the phase of word is important in the process of the creation or initiation of things.

Whereas in man we see things as if they are on a time-line where we can place several positions and align them with each stage representing a point on the line. Thus, we have seconds, minutes, hours, and days on a space from one point to another.

The concept of time is linear in humans.

Thought Idea	Word	Fulfillment	Manifestation Visibility
1	2	3	4 →

Man's problem is that he believes that things begin to exist at the moment they are visible or manifested before him, whereas they were already there in the spiritual and invisible.

21

In the process of creation, time is not linear in God but punctual.

Ultimately, in God's chronology, the four steps are not aligned successively or progressively in a timeline. They all happen at the same moment or in an instant because time is not linear with God. He is outside of time; the beginning and the end are at the same moment. He is Eternal, excluding any notion of time.

For God, time is like a point, a moment, or a precise instant where everything is done. When God says something, he sees its beginning and its completion, better yet its accomplishment and its visibility. God sees things in their spiritual and invisible reality. He is not affected by their visibility (or manifestation) because he is outside of time. He who sees the invisible does not need to see them in the visible; visibility does not change the fact that these things exist.

When God says something, he sees its beginning and its completion, better yet its fulfillment and visibility.

This is also the reason why when God thinks of something, it has started, finished, been accomplished, and is visible, whereas from the perspective of man, there is the passage of time and sometimes it can be long.

Let God alone, be recognized as true and every man as a liar. The truth is God's and not men[2].

Thought (decision)

Word ( ) **Accomplishment**

Visibility or manifestation

It must also be said that God is not affected by the visibility of things because he himself is invisible. What he has said, he sees even if we as humans do not see it. That is why in the spiritual dimension, he asks us to walk by faith (invisible) and not by sight (visible).

---

2. **Romans 3: 4 AMP** *"Certainly not! Let God be found true (as He will be), though every person be found a liar, just as it is written (in scripture), that you may be justified in your words, and prevail when you are judged (by sinful men).*

"For we walk by faith, not by sight." **2 Corinthians 5: 7.**

We cannot operate in creation and production prayers if we are moved by the visible.

We must therefore strive to operate based on the invisible rather than the visible. Faith leads us to live according to the invisible things, even if their visibility will be slow to manifest.

The man of faith is one who functions in the invisible, not the visible. I would not want my faith to be moved or affected by the things I see.

God is present, not past or future.

When God presents himself to Moses, he does so as "I am", not as a past or a future but as the one who is at that moment. Again, an identification of God outside of time, as on a point in the present.

"I AM WHO I AM; and He said, "you shall say this to the Israelites, 'I AM has sent me to you." **Exodus 3: 14 AMP.**

24
Two perspectives in counting time

"For a thousand years in thy sight Are but as yesterday when it is past, And as a watch in the night." **Psalms 90: 4**

"For a thousand years in Your sight Are like yesterday when it is past, Or as a watch in the night." **Psalms 90: 4 AMP.**

When the Bible says that for God, 1000 years is like a day, it is simply stating that God doesn't count time like we do because He is outside of time; He is Eternal. He is not subject to time, and therefore not affected by it. Thus, there is no chronology of events in His mode of operation, everything is done instantaneously in thought, will accomplishment, and visibility.

This is also why God asks us to believe that we have received what we ask for (divine perspective) and we will see it fulfilled (human perspective).

It is man who has the notion of chronology (time), whereas God is outside of time.

The divine perspective is outside of time, everything happens simultaneously, not in a linear fashion.

"Therefore, I say unto you, All things whatsoever ye pray and ask for, believe that ye receive them, and ye shall have them." **Mark 11: 24**

If you believe you have received it, it will be given to you.

If you doubt in your heart, it means you haven't received anything.

- Faith and reception occur at the same time.
- Faith and fulfillment happen at the same time.
- What you ask for, is received when you believe, not when you see.

In the divine perspective, everything happens simultaneously, whereas in the human perspective, things appear chronological. But only God asks us to walk according to His perspective so that we can work and operate as He does.

This ensures that we are never affected by the visibility of things, we walk by faith, not by sight.

We must match the timing of our belief with the timing of the quality of our faith declaration.

Living in faith means seeing nothing at the time we believe. This is well captured in the Word of Life version, which states.

"For we live by faith and yet see nothing." **2 Corinthians 5:** **7**

26
The prophet functions in the invisible

God gives him the ability to access invisible things.

"For He spoke, and it was done; He commanded, and it stood fast." **Psalms 33: 9 AMP.**

We must get used to declaring things, ordering them, and speaking to them if we want to see them happen not only in our lives and destinies but also in our environment.

When God wanted to begin the work of man's deliverance from sin after the fall of the first Adam, He made the declaration, the reflection of the thought or decision of the plan for man's redemption. He said, *"I will put enmity between you and the woman, between your seed and her seed: she shall bruise your head and you shall bruise her heel."*

When God decides or has a thought, He is speaking about what He has resolved so that the gestation will continue.

This is one of the reasons why the Bible is full of declarations, words, ordinances and promises of God that reflect His thoughts or decisions already accomplished.

27
The material world and the spiritual world.

This is the moment to recall the existence of two worlds, the material and the spiritual. Creation takes place on both levels.

We exist with God before the foundation of the world.

"Even as he chose us in him before the foundation of the world, that we should be holy and without blemish before him in love: having foreordained us unto adoption as sons through Jesus-Christ unto himself, according to the good pleasure of his will" **Ephesians 1: 4 - 5**

If God chose us before the foundation of the world, it means we existed before the beginning of the world, and our manifestation only came later for Adam in Genesis and for the others at the time of their birth. We should therefore distinguish between the existence of things on one hand and their manifestation on the other.

In God, things are visible in their spiritual aspect. Man believes that things that are not visible do not exist and cannot affect him. That's why some people believe that because they don't see God, He does not exist.

Existence comes before visibility or manifestation. Visibility or manifestation does not guarantee existence and truth.

Since God is invisible, He wanted to give us His image through Jesus-Christ, as the Apostle Paul confirms when he says, *"Christ is the visible image of the invisible God."* **(Colossians 1: 15).**

29
APPLICATION

1. Start by speaking about "what you want to do, calling it into existence."
2. Call your project by its name to get it started.
3. Bring your ideas and thoughts to life through the words you speak.

30

CHAPTER 2

THE POWER OF THE NAME AS WORD/ THE NAMING PROCESS

It is interesting to note that in the beginning, God completed each creation by giving it a name to the point that there was an identity between the creation and the name it bore. So, there is nothing that God created without giving it a name. It was part of the creation process, if not the signature of everything God created.

Look at the first day, for example, when God said, *"Let there be light. And there was light. God saw that the light was good; and God separated the light from the darkness. God called the light day, and he called the darkness night. So, there was evening and there was morning: that was the first day."* **Genesis 1: 3 - 5.**

God gives a name to his work and determines its characteristics to the point of establishing an identity between, for example, light and day and darkness and night.

There is an identity between the name and what is named or called. This is the principle of the identity of the name with the thing or person that bears it.

When you say someone's name, you are talking about their identity. The name reflects the identity as stated by Reverend Tony Evans in his book The Power of Jesus Names.

The name is a word spoken about someone, about their

life and about something. In this respect, the name as a word has as much power as the word or message it carries.

Whenever the name is pronounced, the word is at the same time proclaimed or declared on the life of the person or thing named. There are so many examples in the Bible where God not only gave the name but also changed it according to the mission, vision or calling on the life of the person. As much as every word must be taken seriously, so must the name.

"You shall not use the name of the Lord your God to deceive, for the Lord will not leave him unpunished who uses his name to deceive." **Exodus 20: 7 - 8**

"You shall not take a false oath by my name, for you would profane the name of your God. I am the Lord." **Leviticus 19: 12.**

God takes the name very seriously because he knows the power it carries or its impact on someone or something's life.

God continues to speak to him: *"you shall no longer be called Abram. Your new name shall be Abraham. For I am making you the father of many peoples"* **Genesis 17: 5**

The name contains a very important spiritual heritage and can carry a message from generation to generation.

Beyond this heritage, it has power over its bearer. It is first a word before being an identity in relation to the person. Thus, for example, **the name of Abraham says to the generations to come that I am your father, I have transmitted to you the covenantal blessings that I received from my Father, you are also beneficiaries.**

The name is a spiritual and legal heritage whenever it is spoken.

The name is also an element of identification in relation to filiation or membership of a group or people. Through the name you can find out where someone comes from. As such, the name always connects you, whether you want it to or not. If you are named after Hitler, everyone will want to know why you were given his name.

What about if you have the name Graham, Bush...

The name is an indicator of your source and origin.

In conclusion, naming is a very important and momentous act of creation in life and should be taken seriously. It can affect a destiny positively or negatively.

For example, in Israel names were given to express the hopes and dreams of the parents. So, parents choose names to reflect what their sons were destined to become, as Dr Tony Evans again demonstrates.

God never separated creation from its name and there is nothing He created without giving it a name because the two are intimately linked.

Speaking of the name, it is important to look at what the power of the name of Jesus-Christ teaches us to better understand what we are saying about the power of the name as a word.

The power of the name of Jesus-Christ.

The reading of **Isaiah 9: 5** and the following verses in several Bible versions will help us better understand the scope and power of the name, especially that of Jesus-Christ.

"For to us a Child shall be born, to us a Son shall be given; And the government shall be upon His shoulder, And His name shall be called Wonderful Counselor, Mighty God, Everlasting Father, Prince of Peace." **AMP.**

« For to us a child is born, to us a son is given; and the government shall be upon his shoulder, and his name shall be called Wonderful Counselor, Mighty God, Everlasting Father, Prince of Peace." **ESV.**

God gave the name to Jesus-Christ because He knew His mission and power. This name was much more focused on His mission than just a means of identification.

It contains power and might within it and, above all, determines how its holder functions, exercises dominion and power, and finally how everything under the earth is subjected to it.

The name of Jesus saves. *"And there is salvation in no one else, for there is no other name under heaven given among men by which we must be saved."* **Acts 4: 12**

He heals and has the power to cast out demons. The latter know that his name has power and that is why they obey and run away.

Furthermore, His name saves from sins. (**Matthew 1: 21** she shall bring forth a son, and thou shalt call his name Jesus; and he shall save his people from their sins); he gives forgiveness of sins. (All the prophets testify of him that whoever believes in him receives forgiveness of sins through his name.) **Acts 10: 43**

The implication is that those who come in the name of Jesus-Christ also carry his authority and are therefore identified with him, for it must be said again that **the name has legal and spiritual significance because it gives rights to the one who bears or uses it.**

By coming in the name of Jesus or by acting in his name, we are entitled to the powers and authorities that belong to him, which are linked to his name.

Whenever someone quotes Jesus-Christ, he is saying that he is wonderful, and he will contemplate his wonderful works. He is the Counsellor, and he will bene- fit from his advice and the decisions of his council. He is a strong and powerful God so he will experience his power in all areas including his strength in everything. He is the Father of eternity, he will enjoy the sonship, and he is the Prince of peace and he will give him his peace which surpasses all understanding. In short, he is everything that is written about his person, his authority, his power, his might...

Everything obeys him because everything that is attached to his person as God, summarized in his name.

Whoever calls on the name of the Lord will be saved[3], just means whoever calls on the person of Jesus (the one who saves, the one who heals, the one who delivers, the one who forgives sins, the one who cleanses, the one in whom there is salvation ...) will be saved or will live all that this name means.

His name is therefore the spiritual and legal summary of this description and these characteristics.

You only have to say in the name of Jesus-Christ to live and experience all that he is there to bring to us. God

---

3. **Romans 10: 13** *"For "everyone who calls on the name of the Lord will be saved."*

has simplified things for us by condensing everything into His name.

There is no difference between the name and the person of Jesus.

We must know that legally the demons obey us in the name of Jesus because they know they have no power over Him and therefore they must deal with Him, (His authority, power, and might). As said before, the name is the summary or better the synthesis of the person or the characteristics of the person.

It is a spiritual law that the name carries power as a word, the bearer of which has the legal right to it.

Thus, the sons of Sheva[4] could not legally use the name of Jesus because they were not his disciples. It was declared to the disciples; in my name, they will cast out demons but not to anyone.

You have no legal right to use that name, Paul can because he is his disciple. We listen and obey those who have the right to use the name but not you, they must

---

4. **Acts 19: 13-15** *"Then some of the itinerant Jewish exorcists undertook to invoke the name of the Lord Jesus over those who had evil spirits, saying, "I adjure you by the Jesus whom Paul proclaims." Seven sons of a Jewish high priest named Sceva were doing this. But the evil spirit answered them, "Jesus I know, and Paul I recognize, but who are you?"*

have thought!

Demons and everything else know the powers and authority of the name of Jesus and that is why they obey. This is according to the scripture which says:

*"Therefore, God has highly exalted him and bestowed on him the name that is **above every name**, so that at the name of Jesus **every knee should bow**, in heaven and on earth and under the earth, and **every tongue confess** that Jesus-Christ is Lord, to the glory of God the Father."* **Philippians 2: 9-11**

When you mention the name of Jesus, legally, the spiritual world understands that it is about the person of Jesus-Christ himself as the name carries as much power as the person himself. It is also clear that the name has an impact or power in the spiritual world, but God has given Jesus' name much more so that every knee should bow in heaven and on earth and under the earth, and every tongue confess that Jesus-Christ is Lord.

Everyone or anything that hears the name of Jesus-Christ will bow. If you compare the above text with **Romans 14: 11** (borrowed from **Isaiah 45: 23**[5]), you will

---

5. **Isaiah 45: 23** *"By myself I have sworn; from my mouth has gone out in righteousness a word that shall not return: 'To me every knee shall bow, every tongue shall swear allegiance."*

realize that what is said about Jesus is exactly what Paul says to the Philippians about His name, to establish that the name carries the same power as the person.

For it is written, *"As I live, says the Lord, every knee* **shall bow to me***, and every tongue shall confess to God."* **Romans 14: 11**

The disciples understood the same principle, and indeed they soon invoked it when they found themselves before someone in need of healing. Knowing that it is Jesus-Christ who heals and who has the power to do so, and that he himself had said that those who believe will exercise this power. They were quick to say, *"But Peter said, "I have no silver and gold, but what I do have I give to you. In the name of Jesus-Christ of Nazareth, rise up and walk!"* **Acts 3: 6**

As the people did not quite understand that this was only normal for the one who believes, he goes on to explain it in even clearer terms in **Acts 3: 16** by saying that it was through faith in his name that his name strengthened this man whom they saw and knew. In other words, he meant that it was through faith in Jesus-Christ that he strengthened the man…

In the name of Jesus is not a formula, it is the power and might that the name carries.

41

The spiritual world knows the power of the name because it also knows the power of the word, it respects and obeys the word summarized in the name.

If you read the scriptures carefully, you will realize that Jesus manifested during His ministry all that was contained and summarized in His name. There is not enough time to go through all the achievements and accomplishments of Jesus-Christ related to his name.

If we understand these principles, then we can benefit from all the powers and attributes of the name of Jesus-Christ. I call upon him as Immanuel[6] during difficult times, he joins me in my troubles no matter what situation I face, what enemies I face, what enemies are before me.

"The birth of Jesus-Christ is not only the introduction of our Savior into the world but also the introduction of the promise of victory and his presence in the midst of the difficult situations that we know so well."[7]

So, we can call upon God in every situation, and He will manifest Himself according to His name and attributes.

---

6. **Matthew 1: 22 - 23** *"All this took place to fulfill what the Lord had spoken by the prophet: "Behold, the virgin shall conceive and bear a son, and they shall call his name Immanuel" (which means, God with us).*

7. The Power of the Jesus Names, Tony Evans, p285.

I like this parallelism established by Tony Evans in his book[8] which brings out the names of God in correlation with Jesus-Christ and so every time we say Jesus, it is for example:

- Immanuel: God with us in every situation
- Elohim, God the creator of all things knowing that it is Christ Jesus who created all things according to **Colossians 1: 16**[9]
- The great I am, which Jesus takes up in John when he speaks of Abraham.
- Jehovah Nissi, which means our banner and victory and we know that Jesus has overcome the world according to **John 16: 33**[10].

Jehovah Rohi which means God is our shepherd. Jesus came to us as the good shepherd and his sheep know his voice.[11]

---

8. The Power of the Jesus Names, Tony Evans, p302-303.

9. **Colossians 1: 15 - 17** *"He is the image of the invisible God, the firstborn of all creation. For by him all things were created, in heaven and on earth, visible and invisible, whether thrones or dominions or rulers or authorities—all things were created through him and for him. And he is before all things, and in him all things hold together."*

10. **John 16: 33** *"I have said these things to you, that in me you may have peace. In the world you will have tribulation. But take heart; I have overcome the world."*

11. **John 10: 4, 11** *"When he has brought out all his own, he goes before them, and the sheep follow him, for they know his voice. I am the good shepherd. The good shepherd lays down his life for the sheep."*

- Jehovah Sabaoth. This name refers to him as the Lord God of hosts. Jesus said that he could call 12 legions of angels to fight on his behalf. He commands the armies of heaven.[12]
- El Elyon, the God who is most high and mighty. Jesus is seated at the right hand of the Father in the highest place.[13]
- El Shaddai, God Almighty. Jesus is the Almighty God.[14]

The name is the vehicle of the authority contained in the message of its bearer.

---

12. **Matthew 26: 53** *"Do you think that I cannot appeal to my Father, and he will at once send me more than twelve legions of angels?"*

13. **Ephesians 1: 20 - 21** *"that he worked in Christ when he raised him from the dead and seated him at his right hand in the heavenly places, far above all rule and authority and power and dominion, and above every name that is named, not only in this age but also in the one to come."*

14. **Apocalypse 1: 8** *"I am the Alpha and the Omega," says the Lord God, "who is and who was and who is to come, the Almighty."*

I also endorse this statement by Dr Jean Claude Ntumba: "*all authority, all power, all that was in Jesus-Christ is found in his name.*"[15]

Moses and the power of his name

"When the child grew older, she brought him to Pharaoh's daughter, and he became her son. She named him Moses, "Because," she said, "I drew him out of the water." **Exodus 2: 10**

First of all, it should be made clear that it was not Moses' mother who gave him the name, but Pharaoh's daughter who said that it was because he was brought out of the water (taken out of). She thought that the name was just related to Moses' past, that it was just a reminder that he had been drawn from the waters, a reminder of how Moses was saved from the waters.

However, his name also had a very prophetic future significance because Moses was not only pulled out of the waters, but he got out of all other situations not only related to the waters in his future:

---

15. See Comprendre le mystère des villes refuges, Docteur Jean Claude Ntumba, Ecole Biblique de la Compréhension, p14., 2020.

1. Moses brought the people of Israel out of Egypt.[16]
2. Moses took the people out of Pharaoh's slavery.[17]
3. Moses overcame the waters of the Red Sea.[18]
4. Moses overcame all the problems associated with the waters.[19]
5. Moses overcame the lack of water in the desert.[20]

---

16. **Exodus 3: 10** *"Come, I will send you to Pharaoh that you may bring my people, the children of Israel, out of Egypt."*

17. **Exodus 3: 12** *"He said, "But I will be with you, and this shall be the sign for you, that I have sent you: when you have brought the people out of Egypt, you shall serve God on this mountain."*

18. **Exodus 14: 21 – 23** *"Then Moses stretched out his hand over the sea, and the Lord drove the sea back by a strong east wind all night and made the sea dry land, and the waters were divided. And the people of Israel went into the midst of the sea on dry ground, the waters being a wall to them on their right hand and on their left. The Egyptians pursued and went in after them into the midst of the sea, all Pharaoh's horses, his chariots, and his horsemen."*

19. **Exodus 15: 23** *"When they came to Marah, they could not drink the water of Marah because it was bitter; therefore, it was named Marah."*

20. **Exodus 17: 3 – 7** *"But the people thirsted there for water, and the people grumbled against Moses and said, "Why did you bring us up out of Egypt, to kill us and our children and our livestock with thirst?" So Moses cried to the Lord, "What shall I do with this people? They are almost ready to stone me." And the Lord said to Moses, "Pass on*

6. Moses overcame all the complicated situations he faced.

Just because you don't know the power of your name doesn't mean it won't work. Just because he who gave you the name did not know the extent of its power does not mean that it will not act.

There is not enough time to talk about Abram, whose name was changed to Abraham to conform to his new mission and especially to his destiny as the father of faith, whose descendants would constitute multitudes that he was unable to count, as many as the stars of the sky. It should be the same with Sarai, who became Sarah, his wife, to conform and adapt to her husband's new calling and mission. See **Genesis 17: 4, 15** "Behold, my covenant is with you, and you shall be the father of a multitude of nations. And God said to Abraham, "As for Sarai your wife, you shall not call her name Sarai, but Sarah shall be her name."

---

before the people, taking with you some of the elders of Israel, and take in your hand the staff with which you struck the Nile, and go. Behold, I will stand before you there on the rock at Horeb, and you shall strike the rock, and water shall come out of it, and the people will drink." And Moses did so, in the sight of the elders of Israel. And he called the name of the place Massah and Meribah, because of the quarreling of the people of Israel, and because they tested the Lord by saying, "Is the Lord among us or not?"

What about Jacob (the one who heeled: he held the heel of his older brother Esau at birth) whose name was changed by God to conform to his new destiny and especially to carry the prophetic message of God's overcomer, the one who fought with God and overcame. See **Genesis 32: 28** "And he said, 'Your name shall no longer be Jacob, but you shall be called Israel; for you have fought with God and with men and have prevailed.

Whenever God wanted to change a man's history or destiny, He also changed his name. This is the spiritual principle, for the name carries the power of the message it conveys, it is worth its meaning.

In the spiritual world, the name is worth the message it carries.

The importance of Peter's name

To mark Simon's destiny, Jesus also changed his name in order to make him the one on whom he would build his church, in other words, the rock on which he would found his church.

"And I tell you, you are Peter, and on this rock, I will build my church, and the gates of hell shall not prevail against it." **Matthew 16: 18**

It should be remembered that Simon was a very common name of the time and meant one who is heard. But according to the mission that Jesus was going to give to this apostle, father of the Church, he was going to call him Peter (petra, rock).

Peter's name, therefore, also conveys his mission to be the rock of the Church. He is the one through whom the Church had its beginnings on the day of Pentecost, as reported in the Acts of the Apostles.

The power of her husband's name

As much as a name contains a spiritual heritage, it is also important to take seriously the fact that a woman bears her husband's name following marriage. Let us remember that the name has a heritage and the fact of becoming one flesh with her husband. It is therefore normal and even recommendable that a woman also bears her husband's name. This act also has a spiritual significance insofar as the two will share the same legal or spiritual heritage. It is possible to carry a patrimony coming from the name of your family that may conflict with your new family.

Logically, the woman could also carry the heritage of her family's name into her new family, but in some cases, this can cause problems because it does not allow for an attachment to her new family.

The name is also the means of identifying with her husband, of sharing the same powers, or rather the same blessings attached to the name. God said to Abraham, "*I will make your name great*".

It is true that many legislations leave the option for the wife to bear her husband's name if she wishes. The fact that a woman does so is a sign of attachment, submission, belonging, union, and identification with her husband. It is therefore not an obligation, but I believe that for other women, doing so could be a cause of detachment from a heritage for an attachment to the heritage of her new family. For some women, taking her husband's name may be a release from the effects of a bad spiritual heritage. It is up to you to look at your life and see if it is beneficial for you to carry your husband's name. May God enlighten you and know that God himself has already changed the names of servants.

Dr Myles Munroe[21] demonstrated in one of his posts that some women have had problems in their marriages because they would not give up their family names. He talks about a famous woman who decided to keep her family name, not to give it up, but whose husband was involved in several scandals and infidelities. I believe

---

21. The change of name Myles Munroe, (2) Why a Woman Must CHANGE HER NAME AFTER MARRIAGE - Myles Munroe (MUST WATCH NOW!!!) - YouTube

that since the name has a spiritual significance, this is possible because the name also indicates your source or origin. In the same way that a name carries greatness, so does the reverse.

I have a new name.

"He who has an ear, let him hear what the Spirit says to the churches. To the one who conquers I will give some of the hidden manna, and I will give him a white stone, with a new name written on the stone that no one knows except the one who receives it." **Revelation 2: 17**

"The nations shall see your righteousness, and all the kings your glory, and you shall be called by a new name that the mouth of the Lord will give." **Isaiah 62: 2**

So much so that the name carries important spiritual baggage. It is also changed when we choose to become Christians. We need to read the above passages in a present and future perspective to realize that we will receive or have received a new name when we become a Christian. God gives us a new name, and I believe that if our names are written in the book of life, it is that name. This is not a doctrine; it is just my personal interpretation of the text.

Would God agree to inscribe us in his register with a name that may carry a message contrary to the newness of life that he brings to us? As it is written, if anyone is in Christ, he is a new creation, and old things have passed away, and behold, all things have become new.

2 Corinthians 5: 17.

"The one who conquers, I will make him a pillar in the temple of my God. Never shall he go out of it, and I will write on him the name of my God, and the name of the city of my God, the new Jerusalem, which comes down from my God out of heaven, and my own new name." **Revelation 3 : 12**

This again highlights the importance of the name because it is more than just an identifier; it is a prophetic message and has a corresponding spiritual background.

We also realize, for example, that even though Elijah was taken up and no longer experiences death, in other words he is in paradise awaiting the resurrection. God speaks of John the Baptist as Elijah who was to come. The name Elijah here is a spiritual baggage; God meant that John the Baptist will have the same characteristics as Elijah. He will carry the same spiritual bag- gage as Elijah, who was like him.

52
How to change the name and empty it of its negative content?

As naming is a spiritual act, it is possible that we can change our names on God's recommendation as was the case with Abraham, Jacob, and many other examples in the Bible. It should be noted that in the case of Abram and Sarah, God instructed that they could bear their new names, and as we shall see later, they were called such by their contemporaries.

"No longer shall your name be called Abram, but your name shall be Abraham, for I have made you the father of a multitude of nations. I will make you exceedingly fruitful, and I will make you into nations, and kings shall come from you." **Genesis 17: 5 - 6**

Then God said to Abraham, *"And God said to Abraham, "As for Sarai your wife, you shall not call her name Sarai, but Sarah shall be her name. I will bless her, and moreover, I will give you a son by her. I will bless her, and she shall become nations; kings of peoples shall come from her."* **Genesis 17: 15 - 16.**

After these passages, wherever Abram and Sarai are mentioned, they are always referred to as Abraham and Sarah. God himself will change the way he calls them.[22]

---

22. **Genesis 17: 15 - 19** *"And God said to Abraham, "As for Sarai your*

Not only God but also the angels have acted to change the names of Abram and Sarai and call them that.[23]

The best way to empty a name of its content is to use the new name for a new message, a new spiritual and legal baggage that is effective and real.

"Then he said, "Your name shall no longer be called Jacob, but Israel, for you have striven with God and with men, and have prevailed." Then Jacob asked him, "Please tell me your name." But he said, "Why is it that you ask my name?" And there he blessed him." **Genesis 32: 28 - 29**

"And God said to him, "Your name is Jacob; no longer shall your name be called Jacob, but Israel shall be your name." So he called his name Israel. And God said to him, "I am God

---

wife, you shall not call her name Sarai, but Sarah shall be her name. I will bless her, and moreover, I will give you a son by her. I will bless her, and she shall become nations; kings of peoples shall come from her." Then Abraham fell on his face and laughed and said to himself, "Shall a child be born to a man who is a hundred years old? Shall Sarah, who is ninety years old, bear a child?" And Abraham said to God, "Oh that Ishmael might live before you!" God said, "No, but Sarah your wife shall bear you a son, and you shall call his name Isaac. I will establish my covenant with him as an everlasting covenant for his offspring after him."

23. **Genesis 18: 9 - 10** *"They said to him, "Where is Sarah your wife ?" And he said, "She is in the tent." The Lord said, "I will surely return to you about this time next year, and Sarah your wife shall have a son." And Sarah was listening at the tent door behind him."*

Almighty: be fruitful and multiply. A nation and a company of nations shall come from you, and kings shall come from your own body." God called him Israel. **Genesis 35: 10 - 11**

We continue to see in the following that Jacob's children and even other callers continue to call him Jacob when God had already changed his name. Why do they continue to call him by his old name?

We will see later that Jesus continued to call him Jacob when he is talking about him in God's quotation of Abraham, Isaac, and Jacob. How is it that the new name Abraham appears but not Jacob?

"And at the time of the offering of the oblation, Elijah the prophet came near and said, "O Lord, **God of Abraham, Isaac, and Israel***, let it be known this day that you are God in Israel, and that I am your servant, and that I have done all these things at your word."* **1 Kings 18: 36**

The prophet Elijah quotes this covenant formula with the new names of Abram and Jacob, while Jesus and the apostles quote it with the old name Jacob in the New Testament. In this formula each patriarch represents a memorial in the covenants made. So, Jacob represents the one who did not deserve, but God made a covenant with him but it is just a reminder, the name has already been emptied of its content. Abraham prophesied that he will be the father of a multitude, whereas Jacob was already a conqueror that's why he got the name. Abraham was going to become the father of a multitude. When you hear Jacob, it is just as a reminder of what God has done.

"And as for the dead being raised, have you not read in the book of Moses, in the passage about the bush, how God spoke to him, saying, 'I am the God of Abraham, and the God of Isaac, and the God of Jacob'?" **Mark 12: 26**.

APPLICATION

Take a sheet of paper and write or use a writing surface.

1. I write the name I give to my destiny (for example: the one who prepares the way of the Lord, the light of the world, the reserve of the Lord, the father of many...)
2. I write names or give names to my life projects in all areas such as: marriage, libala ya lokumu (marriage of honor from lingala[24]), buying my first house, named it Genesis for example...
3. I pray by calling things or projects by their found names like "Libala ya lokumu" be blessed and that the financial means are available! Bless Genesis impacts negatively on my life.
4. Am I experiencing the negative effects of my family name in my marriage?
5. Is it a blessing or pride to bear my husband's name? If I decide to carry my husband's name.

---

24. One of the four national languages of the Democratic Republic of Congo.

CHAPTER 3

COMMAND BY THE WORD

And God said: "*Let there be light!*" **Genesis 1: 3**

Just as God commanded light to exist, so man, created in his own image and restored by Jesus-Christ, has the power to command things visible, invisible, material, and spiritual.

God's work in the beginning was essentially to give orders. He called light into existence, and so it was. He commanded the atmosphere of heaven, the light to come to earth.

God created man in his image to act like him. That is why Jesus could say my Father acts, so do I.

"But Jesus answered them, "My Father is working until now, and I am working." **John 5: 17**

Like him, God has endowed us with the word or voice to communicate between us and nature, but also to operate like him, to give orders. We cannot say that we are created in the image of God and refuse to act like him.

59
The word is the expression of orders and the exercise of authority.

We have the word or voice to command, to order things visible, invisible, physical, and spiritual. In the name of Jesus-Christ, the perfect image of God, we can thus command things, both in heaven and on earth.

Creation responds to God's command and order in the name of Jesus-Christ, for whatever we bind on earth will be bound in heaven[25].

Nature and creation are recipients of God's commands. God gave man his identity to continue to act as such. From the book of the beginning of all things to the book of the end, it is all about power, authority and command. From **Genesis 1: 28**[26] to **Matthew 28: 18 - 20**[27] to

---

25. **Matthew 18: 18** *"Truly, I say to you, whatever you bind on earth shall be bound in heaven, and whatever you loose on earth shall be loosed in heaven."*

26. **Genesis 1: 28** *"And God blessed them. And God said to them, "Be fruitful and multiply and fill the earth and subdue it and have dominion over the fish of the sea and over the birds of the heavens and over every living thing that moves on the earth."*

27. **Matthew 28: 18 - 20** *"And Jesus came and said to them, "All authority in heaven and on earth has been given to me. Go therefore and make disciples of all nations, baptizing them in the name of the Father and of the Son and of the Holy Spirit, teaching them to observe all that I have commanded you. And behold, I am with you always, to*

Matthew 10: 7 - 8[28].

It is all about power and authority. So, when it comes to exercising this, there is nothing to do but give orders and commands.

Nothing or no environment can resist the Word of God or the voice of God, especially when it comes to a given command.

There are men in the Bible who used this power to command and give orders in many circumstances of time and place.

There is no need to recall the story of the patriarch Joshua, who did not hesitate to order the sun and the moon to suspend their courses as reported in his book in **chapter 10: 12-14.**

"At that time Joshua spoke to the Lord in the day when the Lord gave the Amorites over to the sons of Israel, and he said in the sight of Israel, "Sun, stand still at Gibeon, and moon, in the Valley of Aijalon." And the sun stood still, and the moon stopped, until the nation took vengeance on their enemies. Is this not written in the Book of Jashar? The sun stopped in the midst of heaven and did not hurry to set for about a whole day. There has been no day like it before or

---

the end of the age."

28. **Matthew 10: 7 - 8** "And proclaim as you go, saying, 'The kingdom of heaven is at hand.' Heal the sick, raise the dead, cleanse lepers, cast out demons. You received without paying; give without pay."

since, when the Lord heeded the voice of a man, for the Lord fought for Israel."

What about Elijah who prayed to God earnestly that there should be no rain in Israel but at his word, and so it was until he commanded again in the land.

"Now Elijah the Tishbite, of Tishbe in Gilead, said to Ahab, "As the Lord, the God of Israel, lives, before whom I stand, there shall be neither dew nor rain these years, except by my word." **1 Kings 17: 1**

Man has the power to command and order with authority nature and the environment, better still, everything that God has created so that there are changes and expected responses.

The whole life of Jesus-Christ was a reflection and manifestation of this power and authority. Therefore, he threatened the winds, cast out demons, commanded the fig tree to wither, transformed the darkness of men, commanded the sick to be healed, and the dead to rise again.

"Again Jesus spoke to them, saying, "I am the light of the world. Whoever follows me will not walk in darkness, but will have the light of life." **John 8: 12**

Our commands, not that they are directed to the light, but rather to the darkness to drive it out of not only our lives but to our environment. We can also command the darkness to strike our enemies so that they are blinded, that we are invisible in their plans against us.

Furthermore, our commands are also directed at nature, our environment, and things both visible and invisible, both spiritual and physical.

Jesus withdrew the fig tree that did not bear fruit outside its season and the fig tree did not resist the Creator's command even though it was not in season.

The men of Sodom and Gomorrah were struck blind, and the darkness had overtaken them to the point that they could not see.

"And they struck with blindness the men who were at the entrance of the house, both small and great, so that they wore themselves out groping for the door." **Genesis 19: 11**

Actions:

- May our enemies be blinded.
- May those who wish us ill not see us in their plans.
- May God make us invisible to our enemies.
- May God's light drive out the darkness from our lives and our environment.

- May my blessing follow me!
- May my plans succeed!
- May all obstacles before me be destroyed!
- I command money to follow me and be the provision in my vision and projects.
- I command sickness to flee from me and to be far from my life.
- I command the COVID-19 to destroy itself.

Things respond to God's commands. We are his representatives to instruct nature to obey. This is how Moses could give orders to the Red Sea to part in two to allow the People of Israel to cross on dry land. God has given us the power to instruct situations, problems, and circumstances to perform.

1. Assigning times in our favor in battle, see Joshua at Gibeon. "Sun, stop at Gibeon" he commanded.
2. These are prayers that address things and circumstances. In the atmosphere of the Holy Spirit, we speak to heaven, earth, nature, creations, and people.
3. They are prayers that are addressed to us as

well.

4. They are prayers in which we exercise our capacity of divinity, to call things into existence.

5. They are prayers in which we speak to ourselves, "Bless the Lord, O my soul", they are also addressed to our body, our health.

6. All existence is activated by the Word.

7. The Word is the matter of creation of all things.

8. Everything is voice-activated.

9. Prayers of nomination, calling, consecration, designation, prayers of distinction. They are prayers of determination of time or timing of things.

10. They are prayers that affect heaven and earth so that God's will may be done in heaven as well as on earth.

11. They are prayers that affect the earth so that it may be under our dominion.

12. It is a prayer for the earth to produce seed, fruit, everything we need for our life on earth. This prayer is addressed to the trees, to the herbs.

13. Nature and what it contains respond to the

word because it has been formed by the word, it has the same nature as the word; in the composition of nature there is the word, that is why nature always reacts to the word.

14. These are prayers that affect the seasons, days, months and years. They are addressed to the luminaries (Stars, suns, and moons). See the Psalms where David speaks to the luminaries. Joshua speaks to the Sun.

15. Let the heat, the light, the day, and the night be favorable to me and let them hear me. Genesis 1: 14. We cannot worship the stars because they were created to respond to the Creator (Word).

16. These are prayers to the fish, to the animals, they receive our commands, and they can do nothing against us. They obey our voice.

CHAPTER 4

EVERYTHING RESPONDS TO THE WORD

"In the beginning, God created the heavens and the earth. The earth was without form and void, and darkness was over the face of the deep. And the Spirit of God was hovering over the face of the waters. And God said, "Let there be light," and there was light." **Genesis 1: 1 - 3**

Faith moves us to speak, to declare, and not to be silent because when we have it, our word will speak to the time, the circumstances, and the environment to change things.

I believed that's why I spoke.

"Since we have the same spirit of faith according to what has been written, "I believed, and so I spoke," we also believe, and so we also speak," **2 Corinthians 4: 13**

Actions:
"He himself bore our sins in his body on the tree, that we might die to sin and live to righteousness. By his wounds you have been healed." **1 Peter 2: 24**

Here is how I can make this promise effective over my life and especially how it reacts to this word.

I transform the word of God into a voice or a statement so that it activates things.

So, I can say, for example:

I am dead to sin, and it has no impact on me.

I have a righteous life before God through Jesus-Christ, and thank you, Lord, for that.

I am healed of every disease, through the stripes of Jesus-Christ, I am healed of AIDS. AIDS, you have no power over my blood and body. I cast you out of my life and body. My body be healed of all disease from wherever it comes.

1. Command the days and nights, the seasons, the months, and years to bring you success. The times and seasons can be affected, changed so that we can have victory. God can extend the day, the month, the year, the season so that we can have victory.

2. Man's spirit, soul, and body respond to the word.

3. Man can speak to himself and hear the voice and respond to that voice. I can say to myself JPT gets up and prays, you will succeed, don't be discouraged, go for it, run, fly. Be a man of prayer, let prayer be your lifestyle, let the most words from your mouth be prayer, let the longest speech from your mouth be prayer.

4. Man has the power to bless and curse nature and things. I can bless the car, my house, just as I can curse things too...

5. The soul hears the word, it can be encouraged, exhorted by man himself.

6. Psalms 103: 1-3[29]

7. All mountains (problems) hear the voice or word and obey its commands made in faith. Mark 11: 23

8. Nature (trees) serves us and hears our commands. They listen to our commands regard- less of their season. There is no justification for not obeying the voice when it comes to giving provision to God. Mark 11: 14[30]

9. He who believes speaks to all that exists. Mark 9: 23[31]

10. Faith is not silent, it speaks. 2 Corinthians 4 : 13[32];

---

29. "And he said to it, "May no one ever eat fruit from you again." And his disciples heard it." **Mark 11: 14.**

30. "And he said to it, "May no one ever eat fruit from you again." And his disciples heard it." **Mark 11: 14.**

31. "And Jesus said to him, "'If you can'! All things are possible for one who believes." **Mark 9: 23**

32. "Since we have the same spirit of faith according to what has been

11. All things visible and invisible have ears to hear and answer.

12. Nature hears the voice and Word of God

13. Everything that exists has the nature of the Word or the DNA of the Word because it was created by the Word of God

14. Christians can speak to nature (to the mountain, the sun, the moon)

15. When man speaks to nature, God listens and hears[33].

16. Trees (nature) hear the word and obey it.

17. Spirits hear the voice and the word.

18. When man speaks to nature, to the times and circumstances, God listens to the word that is spoken, otherwise God listens to man.

---

written, "I believed, and so I spoke," we also believe, and so we also speak" **2 Corinthians 4: 13.**

33. "At that time Joshua spoke to the Lord in the day when the Lord gave the Amorites over to the sons of Israel, and he said in the sight of Israel, "Sun, stand still at Gibeon, and moon, in the Valley of Aijalon." And the sun stood still, and the moon stopped, until the nation took vengeance on their enemies. Is this not written in the Book of Jashar? The sun stopped in the midst of heaven and did not hurry to set for about a whole day." **Joshua 10: 12 - 13**

"In the beginning was the Word, and the Word was with God, and the Word was God. In the beginning it was with God. All things were made through him, and without him nothing was made that was made." **John 1: 1 - 3**

"In the beginning God created the heavens and the earth. The earth was formless and empty; there was darkness on the face of the deep, and the Spirit of God moved over the waters. And God said, 'Let there be light'; and there was light. And there was light." **Genesis 1: 1 - 3**

To trigger the prayers that we call creation, calling into existence from the invisible to the visible, invention, initiation, or the beginning of things, we need to be in an atmosphere where the Spirit of God is moving because He is the one who carries out the word spoken.

We need to create the conditions for the Spirit to move through worship, the presence of God, who brings glory. It is in this atmosphere that we can pray by proclaiming the words of creation and production. These prayers create new situations in times and circumstances. They bring light where there was darkness, they bring new temperatures, new seasons, they bring days and nights into our lives. They are prayers that affect the luminaries presiding over the days and nights, and the seasons. They bring a new fervor, a warmth to our lives, and they drive out the darkness in our lives. They enlighten our actions.

APPLICATION

- Let the vision and my mission be clear so that I can distinguish things.
- May I see clearly, may light come into my vision, into my work, into my enterprises.
- May the light come into my house so that I may discover the works of darkness.
- May the light come into my home so that I may discover the enemy who hides, or his hidden works.
- May Jesus manifest his light in our family, nation, and society so that we can destroy the works of darkness.

CHAPTER 5

MAKING THINGS THAT ARE INVISIBLE VISIBLE

"By faith we understand that the universe was created by the word of God, so that what is seen was not made out of things that are visible." **Hebrews 11: 3 ESV.**

The things we see were made from those that are invisible.

I declare that invisible promises become a reality in life. Having a life in the invisible world, I give them a life now in the visible. So, I can first name these invisible things, call them to come and respond now in the visible world.

APPLICATION

- I call my wife who already exists in the invisible world; let her come and appear in the visible world, I declare that she will come to me and that I may see her.

- I call all the promises about me, already in the invisible world, that they may now be a reality.

- Mutombo LLC comes into existence, be manifested, buy concessions, build villas and let them be sold; produce results and bring forth profit.

77

...All things are possible to him who believes.

"The hand of the Lord was upon me, and he brought me out in the Spirit of the Lord and set me down in the middle of the valley; it was full of bones. And he led me around among them, and behold, there were very many on the surface of the valley, and behold, they were very dry. And he said to me, "Son of man, can these bones live?" And I answered, "O Lord God, you know." Then he said to me, "Prophesy over these bones, and say to them, O dry bones, hear the word of the Lord. Thus says the Lord God to these bones: Behold, I will cause breath to enter you, and you shall live. And I will lay sinews upon you, and will cause flesh to come upon you, and cover you with skin, and put breath in you, and you shall live, and you shall know that I am the Lord." **Ezekiel 37: 1 - 6 ESV.**

"The hand of the Lord was upon me, and He brought me out in the Spirit of the Lord and set me down in the middle of the valley; and it was full of bones. He caused me to pass all around them, and behold, there were very many [human bones] in the open valley; and lo, they were very dry. And He said to me, "Son of man, can these bones live?" And I answered, "O Lord God, You know." Again He said to me, "Prophesy to these bones and say to them, 'O dry bones, hear the word of the Lord.' Thus says the Lord G od to these bones, 'Behold, I will make breath enter you so that you may come to life. I will put sinews on you, make flesh

grow back on you, cover you with skin, and I will put breath in you so that you may come alive; and you will know that I am the Lord." **Ezekiel 37: 1 - 6 AMP.**

The bones, or what is dead, listen to the voice and word of the man of God or prophet. They could respond to that word. It is important that the word of God be spoken even to things that have no life, to inanimate things, for they have the capacity to listen to God, having in them the composition or material of the Word of God, from which they derive their origin and source.

APPLICATION

1. Can my situation live again?
2. Can what I have lost come back?
3. Can what be dead come back to life?
4. Can life be brought out of something already dead just by its command or word?
5. Can there still be a restoration?
6. Speak to the bones of your life!
7. The bones listen to the word and react to the voice of God and the Prophet.
8. The breath of life waits for the voice to react.
9. Lifeless men listen to the word, so we can address our prayers directly to them by a command.
10. I command a member of my family to be converted; for example, John receives the Word of God and be converted to the Lord Jesus-Christ, be delivered from your vain way of life and be saved.

80

CHAPTER 6

PRAYER AS ADVOCACY

God showed me grace, and I have studied law and hold the equivalent of a master's degree. In addition, I have been a lawyer for more than ten years; and have on several occasions pleaded before courts and tribunals. My knowledge of the law has enriched my understanding of the legal language used in writing.

I have also understood that the Kingdom of God has a legal system or justice to ensure its reign, even its existence.

Furthermore, the Bible is also filled with legal language because God also has a legal system containing an accuser, which other systems call a prosecutor, a lawyer who assists or supports the cases that are brought against his clients and finally, a judge who decides on the cases pending before him.

There is the law of God, especially His word, which is the code or law applicable to the parties or based on which the accused are judged.

"For the Lord is our judge; the Lord is our lawgiver; the Lord is our king; he will save us." **Isaiah 33: 22**

From this text, the LORD exercises the three fundamental powers of a State or Kingdom, namely the judicial, legislative, and executive powers, to better ensure the reign and perpetuity of His Kingdom from generation to generation.

Thus, for example, the system of salvation and redemption is essentially a legal system based on legal principles, the foundation of which is God's law, or rather divine principles. Furthermore, the Bible is filled with legal language to better convey the principles under- lying the judicial power of the Kingdom of God. As an illustration, the Bible speaks of inheritance, adoption, condemnation, freedom, slavery, prison, the accuser, the lawyer, the righteous judge, the last judgment, the Court of Christ...

All legal terms or concepts that imply a full-fledged system of justice or law.

The prosecution

In this system, we can read about Satan as our accuser before God.

"Then he showed me Joshua the high priest standing before the angel of the Lord, and Satan standing at his right hand to accuse him." **Zechariah 3: 1 ESV**.

It should be noted that if he is an accuser, it is because he knows how to use the law of God to that effect; he uses that law obviously to seek to win his case before God. If there is a reason to bring judgment upon you, God will not be able to deviate from His own law because He is the righteous Judge. Praise be to God we have Jesus-Christ as our advocate/lawyer with concrete arguments.

This is why the accuser could question Job's integrity to find a way to incriminate or guilt him. Because in the face of Job's integrity and righteousness, Satan could do nothing but obtain God's permission to touch him. He could not have done anything in the face of Job's integrity and uprightness.

"And the Lord said to Satan, "Have you considered my servant Job, that there is none like him on the earth, a blameless and upright man, who fears God and turns away from evil? He still holds fast his integrity, although you incited me against him to destroy him without reason." Then Satan answered the Lord and said, "Skin for skin! All that a man has he will give for his life." **Job 2: 3 - 4 ESV.**

In other words, if Job was not upright and honest, Satan would not have needed God's permission because sin would have given him the right and access.

"And I heard a loud voice in heaven, saying, "Now the salvation and the power and the kingdom of our God and the authority of his Christ have come, for the accuser of our brothers has been thrown down, who accuses them day and night before our God." **Revelation 12: 10 ESV.**

In view of this passage, the Accuser has a full-time ministry in heaven to accuse night and day the saints whom Christ redeemed at a great price. It is important to note that the brethren were able to defeat him (the accuser) by pleading the Blood of the Lamb, the word of their testimony and the sacrifice of their lives to God. These are important arguments in the pleadings. We will see how to make these arguments in our pleading prayers. Also, it should be noted that when we speak of pleadings, we are generally talking about accusations and therefore we must make the arguments to bring down the accusations of the enemy.

According to this system, the devil is the one who is part of the accuser; he is part of the system of accusation or prosecution before the Court of the Throne of God. He is the accuser not only of men, but also of the saints before God. He is the master of guilt; even before you come to appear before God, he wants to convince you that you are not worthy, therefore you just deserve condemnation. He would like you to live as a condemned man even before God can pronounce the sentence. Also, the judgment on the saints has already been passed, so there is now no condemnation for those who are united to Christ **(Romans 8: 1)**. Whenever the enemy comes with an accusation, He (Christ the Advocate) answers him that the judgment has already been passed since the Cross, where God had judged man through the death of Christ, who had taken our sins. The judgment and sentence had fallen on him. That is why he is also our advocate before God. Because he bore our faults, iniquities and sins, there is no one who knows how to defend our cause as he does, he knows the human condition because he lived in our flesh and body.

It is always the enemy who accuses; every time you feel an accusation in your life, you know that it is another attack, so the enemy is at the base. God convinces him of the sin so that you can repent and at the same time offers forgiveness and peace. If you confess your sin, he is faithful and just to forgive you[35]. I can always tell the difference between the accusation or guilt that comes from the enemy, and the conviction of sin leading to repentance, and the peace that follows that forgiveness.

Beyond the accuser, we would normally have a tribunal, court or jurisdiction before which the accuser comes to present violations, transgressions of the law or divine principles. God is presented as the Judge.

---

35. 1 John 1: 9 *"If we confess our sins, he is faithful and just to forgive us our sins and to cleanse us from all unrighteousness."*

87
The Judge

"God has taken his place in the divine council; in the midst of the gods he holds judgment: "How long will you judge unjustly and show partiality to the wicked?" **Psalm 82: 1 - 2 ESV.**

"God stands in the divine assembly; He judges among the gods (divine beings). How long will you judge unjustly And show partiality to the wicked? Selah." **Psalms 82: 1 - 2 AMP.**

Regarding God as judge, there are many verses that present him as such:

1. God has a council or court in which he judges. **Psalms 82: 1**
2. God from heaven gives sentences. **Psalms 75 : 8 - 9.**[36]
3. God exercises his judgments by fire. **Isaiah 66 : 16**
4. The Lord the righteous judge will give crowns of righteousness to every man. **2 Timothy 4:**

---

36. **Psalm 75: 8 - 9 ESV** *"For in the hand of the Lord there is a cup with foaming wine, well mixed, and he pours out from it, and all the wicked of the earth shall drain it down to the dregs. But I will declare it forever; I will sing praises to the God of Jacob."*

837.

5. God alone is the judge; no man can arrogate to himself that prerogative. **James 4: 12.**[38]

6. The LORD is a judge to decide between men. **Genesis 16: 5**[39]

7. The elder of days will preside over the composition of the judges of the last judgment. **Daniel 7: 9 - 10**[40].

Our God is called the righteous judge because he makes

---

37. **2 Timothy** 4: 8 ESV *"Henceforth there is laid up for me the crown of righteousness, which the Lord, the righteous judge, will award to me on that day, and not only to me but also to all who have loved his appearing."*

38. **James** 4: 12 ESV *"There is only one lawgiver and judge, he who is able to save and to destroy. But who are you to judge your neighbor?"*

39. **Genesis** 16: 5 ESV *"And Sarai said to Abram, "May the wrong done to me be on you! I gave my servant to your embrace, and when she saw that she had conceived, she looked on me with contempt. May the Lord judge between you and me!"*

40. **Daniel** 7: 9 - 10 ESV *"As I looked, thrones were placed, and the Ancient of Days took his seat; his clothing was white as snow, and the hair of his head like pure wool; his throne was fiery flames; its wheels were burning fire. A stream of fire issued and came out from before him; a thousand thousands served him, and ten thousand times ten thousand stood before him; the court sat in judgment, and the books were opened."*

just and fair judgments according to the law. Also, it must be remembered that as King, God also fulfills the judicial powers or a system of justice that ensures justice in His Kingdom, so that violators or law breakers do not go unpunished. It is according to this system of justice that he ensures legality in the Kingdom of God.

The Lawyer

"My little children, I am these things to you so that you may not sin. But if anyone does sin, we have an advocate with the Father, Jesus-Christ the righteous." **1 John 2: 1 ESV.**

The concept of a Lawyer has more meaning than we know in its primary sense. Here it should be seen not only as an advocate but also as a mediator and intercessor. Thus, Jesus-Christ fulfills the role of the one who defends us before God by presenting arguments or proofs of his work on earth. Therefore, in the face of the enemy's accusations of sin, he presents himself as the atoning victim upon whom the punishment or penalty of sin fell. Jesus-Christ pleads his substitution on the cross, he has taken our place, he has made himself sin, he has taken all our sicknesses, our curses, our poverty, better all condemnation and punishment have fallen upon him and therefore God can no longer do anything for those who are in Christ. There is therefore now no condemnation for those who are Christ's according to **Romans 8: 1;**

on the other hand, those who reject His Son will not be beneficiaries of His work of justification at the cross. Jesus-Christ Himself is the quintessential proof of our innocence by substitution and also the argument that God cannot be overthrown against any accusation of the enemy.

What a blessing it is to have believed in Jesus-Christ; no accuser can succeed in a case against one who has faith in Him.

Jesus-Christ is the best lawyer who knows how to defend man because he himself was man, and he knows God because he himself is God.

A good lawyer is one who has had the same training as the judge to know what is needed to pronounce judgment and knows man perfectly because he has suffered or passed through all the situations and conditions of man.

The other aspect of this ministry is that Jesus-Christ is the one who prevents any condemnation against God's elect because He intercedes for them. Paul emphasizes this in the book of Romans when he says:

"Who shall bring any charge against God's elect? It is God who justifies. Who is to condemn? Christ Jesus is the one

who died—more than that, who was raised— who is at the right hand of God, who indeed is interceding for us." **Romans 8: 33 - 34 ESV.**

Jesus-Christ intervenes on our behalf, uses his influence with the Father to defend us, vetoes any decision to condemn us, prays for us to obtain grace and to guarantee us against all evil.

Finally, the ministry of the lawyer is also manifested in his mediation. In some cases, a good lawyer is one who knows how to mediate to facilitate reconciliation or an agreement between the parties.

"For there is one God, and there is one mediator between God and men, the man Christ Jesus, who gave himself as a ransom for all, which is the testimony given at the proper time." **1 Timothy 2: 5 - 6.**

As High Priest, Jesus-Christ plays this mediating role perfectly in that he comes to defend us before God while bringing a perfect sacrifice, which satisfies God, in his own person as the best ransom price. He shed his own blood.[41]

---

41. **Hebrews 9 : 11 - 12** *"But when Christ appeared as a high priest of the good things that have come, then through the greater and more perfect tent (not made with hands, that is, not of this creation) he entered once for all into the holy places, not by means of the blood of goats and calves but by means of his own blood, thus securing an eternal redemption."*

Jesus is, therefore, the advocate par excellence before God; he is the best pleader of our causes before God; no one can beat him because he is God and he was man; he knows the things of God, or he has the nature of God but more than that he was man because he had taken on the human nature.

Pleading Prayers

Having set the scene, it is, therefore, relevant to examine and deepen Isaiah's exhortation to understand what he is saying in his text on pleading. First, it should be noted that the combined definitions of the Larousse and Le Robert dictionaries indicate that pleading is the act of supporting, defending a cause before a judge or in a case pending before a court. It is also to make an argument to be put forward in a case. If we also read the verse in **Isaiah 1: 18** in these different versions.

"Come now, let us reason together, says the Lord: though your sins are like scarlet, they shall be as white as snow; though they are red like crimson, they shall become like wool." **Isaiah 1: 18 ESV.**

"The Lord says, 'Please come, so that we talk about this together. Even if your sins are like a red stain, they will become as white as snow. Even if they are bright red, they

will become like white wool." **Isaiah 1: 18 EASY**.

"Come now, and let's settle this, says the LORD. Though your sins are like scarlet, they will be white as snow. If they are red as crimson, they will become like wool." **Isaiah 1: 18 CEB**.

The prophet Isaiah invites his contemporaries to come and plead with God to change their state. They should come to explain, argue, or plead for a cause or, more importantly, to get God to change things when a decision has already been made, the judgment has already been passed. God promises that if we come to plead, there is a possibility that he will turn the situation in our favor; we should just have arguments to convince him. The question remains, how can a man convince God?

Of course, man can plead before God and argue before Him to change His resolution, decision, and sentences.

Whenever God asks men to plead, it is about condemnation in relation to sin. As Isaiah 1: 18 makes clear, it is important to also read **Isaiah 43: 25 - 26**

"I am he who blots out your transgressions for my own sake, and I will not remember your sins. Put me in remembrance; let us argue together; set forth your case, that you may be proved right." **Isaiah 43: 25 - 26 ESV**.

"I, only I, am He who wipes out your transgressions for My own sake, And I will not remember your sins. Remind Me [of your merits with a thorough report], let us plead and argue our case together; State your position, that you may be proved right." **Isaiah 43: 25 - 26 AMP.**

"I, I am the one who wipes out your rebellious behavior for my sake. I won't remember your sin. Summon me, and let's go to trial together; you tell your story so that you may be vindicated!" **Isaiah 43: 25 - 26 CEB.**

Principles of Pleading Prayers

1. In the pleading, there is often talk of the law, transgression, condemnation of sin and its consequences.

2. In pleading, it is necessary to bring to mind a truth or something important to put on the table, before the court of God.

3. In pleading, God can change His position; it all depends on your argument.

4. We can win our case before God; it depends on how we present ourselves before Him and especially what we use as words (arguments) before Him.

5. Our argument in the presence of God can do something. Also, we have Jesus-Christ and his work as a great argument. This is an unbeatable argument!

6. Pleading is a time to recall, to awaken the memory of God, to bring back to the memory of God His word, His promises, the work of Jesus-Christ, our testimony (what we have done for God, what He has done through us in the Christian life) and our attachment, our sonship.

7. In pleading, we come before a judge; we must bring arguments and evidence to support our case. Jesus-Christ is our argument and evidence.

8. During the advocacy, you list the facts that support your case. You bring the elements for your justification.

9. In the closing argument, you present the case to prove your point.

10. We can count on God's mercy when we come to plead our case before Him.

11. If God asks us to come and explain ourselves before Him, it is because He knows that we can also change His position, and it all depends on what argument, on what word and promises

we bring before Him.

12. Our repentance can reverse the judgment or sentence against us. This causes God to change His mind about us.

A good intercessor is a pleader, he should exercise his ministry in the sense of bringing cases before God so that He changes His position by not imputing to man his sin and its consequences, knowing to use the best argument and the best proof, namely Jesus-Christ.

Some pleaders of the Bible

The Bible gives us stories of some of the pleaders who can inspire us in our intercessory ministry. There are many who have pleaded with God, but we will take just a representative sample to learn from them.

Abraham pleads for the protection of the righteous.

"Then he said, "Oh let not the Lord be angry, and I will speak. Suppose thirty are found there." He answered, "I will not do it, if I find thirty there." He said, "Behold, I have undertaken to speak to the Lord. Suppose twenty are found there." He answered, "For the sake of twenty I will not destroy it." Then he said, "Oh let not the Lord be angry,

and I will speak again but this once. Suppose ten are found there." He answered, "For the sake of ten I will not destroy it." And the Lord went his way, when he had finished speaking to Abraham, and Abraham returned to his place."
Genesis 18: 30 - 33 ESV.

- God revealed to Abraham what he was going to do so that he would know but also intercede.
- The good intercessor doesn't just know what God is going to do but intervenes so that God doesn't exercise His judgment.
- Abraham's intercession saved Lot from the judgment of Sodom and Gomorrah.
- The intercessor or prophet should not only be satisfied that God's judgment will be fulfilled but he prays that God will save and that judgment will not strike.
- The intercessor and prophet seek to convince God to spare the righteous and, above all, to beg God's forgiveness for the people.
- Abraham's goal was to save the righteous from judgment, and God spared them by taking them out of Sodom and Gomorrah so that the unrighteous could not continue to perpetuate the abominations common in those cities.

- God is looking for prophets and intercessors like Abraham who are able to make Him change certain judgments and resolutions.

I am often amazed to see some servants of God being happy because what God had told them is being fulfilled, especially in terms of judgments when they did nothing to prevent this from happening. Jesus-Christ, the intercessor par excellence, prayed on the cross, saying, "*Father, forgive them because they do not know what they are doing*", otherwise no one would have benefited from salvation. The judgment was going to weigh on anyone.

God wants a new generation of servant-intercessors and prophet-intercessors because in these end times there will be everything to make God's wrath stirred up. But as there are still righteous people, His Church, to prevent destruction or death by judgment, there must be a man who raises a wall.

"And I sought for a man among them who should build up the wall and stand in the breach before me for the land, that I should not destroy it, but I found none." **Ezekiel 22 : 30.**

99
Moses pleads for forgiveness.

"... And the Lord said to Moses, "How long will this people despise me? And how long will they not believe in me, in spite of all the signs that I have done among them? **I will strike them with the pestilence and disinherit them, and I will make of you a nation greater and mightier than they."** *But Moses said to the Lord, "Then the Egyptians will hear of it, for you brought up this people in your might from among them, and they will tell the inhabitants of this land. They have heard that you, O Lord, are in the midst of this people. For you, O Lord, are seen face to face, and your cloud stands over them and you go before them, in a pillar of cloud by day and in a pillar of fire by night.* **Now if you kill this people as one man, then the nations who have heard your fame will say, 'It is because the Lord was not able to bring this people into the land that he swore to give to them that he has killed them in the wilderness.'** *And now, please let the power of the Lord be great as you have promised, saying,* **'The Lord is slow to anger and abounding in steadfast love, forgiving iniquity and transgression, but he will by no means clear the guilty, visiting the iniquity of the fathers on the children, to the third and the fourth generation.'** *Please pardon the iniquity of this people, according to the greatness of your steadfast love, just as you have forgiven this people, from Egypt until now."* **Then the Lord said, "I have pardoned, according to your word.** *But truly, as I live, and as all the earth shall be filled with the glory of the Lord"* **Numbers 14: 11 – 21**

- The good intercessor looks not only at the favor God has done him, his position in relation to God, but he takes the place of the one whom God wants to strike with his judgment.
- Moses pleads for the fame of God and the work that God has already done for his people and the testimony of the Gentiles.
- Moses also pleads for God's forgiveness by invoking his word which declares that the Lord is slow to anger and rich in kindness, he forgives iniquity and rebellion; but he does not hold the guilty innocent, and he punishes the iniquity of the fathers on the children to the third and fourth generation. **Numbers 14 : 18**.
- God's Word is an argument we can use to beg for his grace and plead, for he will not break his own word.
- Moses convinced God to change his judgment against the people immediately. He agreed to forgive as he asked.

101
Hezekiah pleads his works.

*"In those days Hezekiah became sick and was at the point of death. And Isaiah the prophet the son of Amoz came to him and said to him, "Thus says the Lord, "**Set your house in order, for you shall die; you shall not recover.**" Then Hezekiah turned his face to the wall and prayed to the Lord, saying, "**Now, O Lord, please remember how I have walked before you in faithfulness and with a whole heart, and have done what is good in your sight.**" And Hezekiah wept bitterly. And before Isaiah had gone out of the middle court, the word of the Lord came to him: "**Turn back, and say to Hezekiah the leader of my people, thus says the Lord, the God of David your father: I have heard your prayer; I have seen your tears.** Behold, I will heal you. On the third day you shall go up to the house of the Lord, and **I will add fifteen years to your life**. I will deliver you and this city out of the hand of the king of Assyria, and I will defend this city for my own sake and for my servant David's sake." And Isaiah said, "Bring a cake of figs. And let them take and lay it on the boil, that he may recover." 2 Kings 20: 1-7, See also Isaiah 38: 1 - 5.*[42]

---

42. **Isaiah 38: 1-5** *"In those days Hezekiah became sick and was at the point of death. And Isaiah the prophet the son of Amoz came to him, and said to him, "Thus says the Lord: Set your house in order, for you shall die, you shall not recover." Then Hezekiah turned his face to the wall and prayed to the Lord, and said, "Please, O Lord, remember how I have walked before you in faithfulness and with a whole heart,*

- God has memories that need to be awakened when we are facing difficult situations. He remembers the works done for him. I can call out the good I have done for God; he will remember it.
- The Prophet who brings you judgment can also bring God's blessing or healing.
- God can change a decision or resolution made against you.

Job pleading for his defense.

"But I would speak to the Almighty, and I desire to argue my case with God. As for you, you whitewash with lies; worthless physicians are you all. Behold, I have prepared my case; I know that I shall be in the right." **Job 13: 3 - 4,18**

Then Job answered and said: "Today also my complaint is bitter; my hand is heavy on account of my groaning. Oh, that I knew where I might find him, that I might come even to his seat! I would lay my case before him and fill my mouth with arguments. I would know what he would answer me and understand what he would say to me." **Job 23: 1-5**

---

and have done what is good in your sight." And Hezekiah wept bitterly. Then the word of the Lord came to Isaiah: "Go and say to Hezekiah, Thus says the Lord, the God of David your father: I have heard your prayer; I have seen your tears. Behold, I will add fifteen years to your life."

- We must have arguments to present to God.
- If you are convinced that you are right, you can present your case to God.
- Come before the throne of God and present your case knowing that you also have an advocate Jesus-Christ who can intervene for you as well.

The Syrian-Phoenician woman pleads for crumbs.

"And from there he arose and went away to the region of Tyre and Sidon. And he entered a house and did not want anyone to know, yet he could not be hidden. But immediately a woman whose little daughter had an unclean spirit heard of him and came and fell down at his feet. Now the woman was a Gentile, a Syrophoenician by birth. And she begged him to cast the demon out of her daughter. And he said to her, "Let the children be fed first, for it is not right to take the children's bread and throw it to the dogs." But she answered him, "Yes, Lord; yet even the dogs under the table eat the children's crumbs." And he said to her, "For this statement you may go your way; the demon has left your daughter." And she went home and found the child lying in bed and the demon gone." **Mark 7: 24 - 30 ESV.**

- Jesus wanted to see the faith of this woman, not to refuse her request but to assess her faith by the arguments presented.

- There are times when we must present arguments even when we have a negative answer from God.
- There are times when we must present arguments even when we have a negative answer from God.
- We can challenge our situation before God, he can change because of the faith we have in the process.

The "pleader" widow and the unfair judge

"He said, "In a certain city there was a judge who neither feared God nor respected man. And there was a widow in that city who kept coming to him and saying, 'Give me justice against my adversary.' For a while he refused, but afterward he said to himself, 'Though I neither fear God nor respect man, yet because this widow keeps bothering me, I will give her justice, so that she will not beat me down by her continual coming.'" And the Lord said, "Hear what the unrighteous judge says. And will not God give justice to his elect, who cry to him day and night? Will he delay long over them? I tell you, he will give justice to them speedily. Nevertheless, when the Son of Man comes, will he find faith on earth?" **Luke 18: 2 - 8 ESV.**

- God defends the right of those who cry out to him night and day.

- God comes to the aid of those who come to dispute before him night and day.
- Faith wants us to stand firm in our defense and to be able to insist when we come before him.

The strongest arguments in our case

*"And they have conquered him by the **blood of the Lamb** and by the **word of their testimony**, for **they loved not their lives even unto death**."* **Revelation 12: 11 ESV.**

The blood of the lamb

To understand the value of the blood of the Lamb, I believe we must go back to the significance of the sacrifice in the temple. In fact, there is not enough time to talk about the victory of the blood. A proper under- standing of the theme would be to first review the practice in the old covenant to understand its significance in this dispensation. Nevertheless, we will circumscribe the notion in the context of the victory of the blood of Jesus-Christ.

The blood of the Lamb is the greatest answer God has given to the world to solve the problem of sin. It is the one that confers the power that has neutralized the power of sin, thus enabling God to reconcile the world to Himself through the blood of His Son shed on the cross. This blood no longer brings God's wrath upon man because of sin, thus guaranteeing peace on earth. So, the letter to the Romans takes him up on it, saying, *"Since, therefore, we have now been justified by his blood, much more shall we be saved by him from the wrath of God."* **Romans 5: 9**

- So we have the forgiveness of our sins through the blood of His Son.

    Colossians 1: 14[43].

- In him we have redemption through his blood, the forgiveness of sins. **Ephesians 1: 7**[44].

- Furthermore, this blood also provides us with the cleansing of our sins. And the blood of Jesus, his Son, cleanses us from all our sins, says John in his first epistle, chapter one and verse 7 in fine. If this is true, the blood of Christ must be even more powerful[45]. This is because it is also the Lamb of God who takes away the sin of the world.

---

43. **Colossians 1: 14** *"in whom we have redemption, the forgiveness of sins."*

44. **Ephesians 1: 7** *"In him we have redemption through his blood, the forgiveness of our trespasses, according to the riches of his grace"*

45. **Hebrews 9: 14** *"how much more will the blood of Christ, who through the eternal Spirit offered himself without blemish to God, purify our conscience from dead works to serve the living God."*

Just as in the ancient sacrificial system, where a lamb or goat had to be sacrificed for the forgiveness of sins, Jesus-Christ was sacrificed on the altar of the cross and shed His precious blood, which thus guarantees the forgiveness and cleansing of sins.

The blood was also the price paid for man's redemption from sin. Peter reminds us that we were not redeemed by corruptible things, silver or gold, but by the precious blood of Christ, as of a lamb without blemish and without spot. No, it was necessary for Christ, as a pure and unblemished lamb, to shed his precious blood as a sacrifice for us. **1 Peter 1: 18 - 19.**[46]

There is no doubt, therefore, that in the face of every accusation, every sin and its consequences that can bring the wrath and justice of God upon us, the blood of Jesus is the strongest argument. The devil therefore cannot resist any invocation or plea calling the blood of Jesus. No one can accuse us, who will accuse God's elect, much more Christ justifies us. The accuser will not stop accusing us by invoking our past and present sins, you have the sledgehammer answer, the blood of the Lamb. This is the argument against any guilt of the

---

46. **1 Peter 1: 18-19** *"knowing that you were ransomed from the futile ways inherited from your forefathers, not with perishable things such as silver or gold, but with the precious blood of Christ, like that of a lamb without blemish or spot"*

enemy.

Whenever the enemy calls for death or death is passing by you, this blood argument paralyses the weapon of death. *"Take a bunch of hyssop and dip it in the blood that is in the basin, and touch the lintel and the two doorposts with the blood that is in the basin. None of you shall go out of the door of his house until the morning."* **Exodus 12: 22.**

There is a terrible power in prayer made by invoking the blood of Jesus or pleading the blood of the Lamb as an argument before our accuser. It always gives victory over the enemy. I have already experienced this personally in my life of prayer and spiritual warfare, including in the face of guilt that prevents us from serving God freely, especially after having sinned. Blood is the weapon par excellence against the guilt resulting from sin.

No one could appear free before God if he or she is not aware of the forgiveness obtained through the precious blood of the Lamb of God who takes away the sin of the world. This is the introduction or presentation that John the Baptist made of Jesus-Christ when he came to be baptized before him.

The awareness of the forgiveness of sin assures us of a victorious attitude, or freedom before the throne of God before whom we must approach every time we come there to pray and worship. No one can approach God without the conviction of forgiveness, or our accuser will invoke our guilt and our past and present sins.

The forgiveness of sins erases the consequences.

"And you, who were dead in your trespasses and the uncircumcision of your flesh, God made alive together with him, having forgiven us all our trespasses, by canceling the record of debt that stood against us with its legal demands. This he set aside, nailing it to the cross. He disarmed the rulers and authorities and put them to open shame, by triumphing over them in him." **Colossians 2: 13 - 15.**

Forgiveness through the blood of Christ also involves many changes and consequences that happen to us.

In particular, it leads to the forgetting of sin by God because he says I will remember your sins no more, as it is written in Hebrews **10: 17** *"then he adds, "I will remember their sins and their lawless deeds no more."*

God blots out transgressions according to **Isaiah 43: 25** *"I, I am he who blots out your transgressions for my own sake, and I will not remember your sins."*

He transforms our condition and our appearance. *"Come now, let us reason together, says the Lord: though your sins are like scarlet, they shall be as white as snow;*

though they are red like crimson, they shall become like wool." **Isaiah 1: 18**

He no longer holds his anger over the consequences of sin. This is echoed by Micah who wonders, *"Who is a God like you, pardoning iniquity and passing over transgression for the remnant of his inheritance? He does not retain his anger forever, because he delights in steadfast love. He will again have compassion on us; he will tread our iniquities underfoot. You will cast all our sins into the depths of the sea."* **Micah 7: 18 - 19**

Since God has forgiven us, we must also forgive others as he did, he instructs us in **Matthew 6: 14 - 15** *"For if you forgive others their trespasses, your heavenly Father will also forgive you, but if you do not forgive others their trespasses, neither will your Father forgive your trespasses."*

The forgiveness of our sins leads us to love others as God loves us despite our sins. *"Therefore, I tell you, her sins, which are many, are forgiven—for she loved much. But he who is forgiven little, loves little."* And he said to her, *"Your sins are forgiven."* **Luke 7: 47 - 48**.

Forgiveness is the manifestation of grace in all its richness. *"In him we have redemption through his blood, the forgiveness of our trespasses, according to the riches of his grace, which he lavished upon us, in all wisdom and insight"* **Ephesians 1: 7 - 8**

Jesus-Christ is our advocate before the Father. Our accuser will face as a pleader the Lamb of God himself. He will never lose a case because he has overcome everything. *"My little children, I am writing these things to you so that you may not sin. But if anyone does sin, we have an advocate with the Father, Jesus-Christ the righteous. He is the propitiation for our sins, and not for ours only but also for the sins of the whole world."* **1 John 2: 1-2.**

No one can accuse us before God. For God's elect, the devil cannot accuse us because he will not be right because Christ died and shed his blood for you.

"Who shall bring any charge against God's elect? It is God who justifies. Who is to condemn? Christ Jesus is the one who died—more than that, who was raised— who is at the right hand of God, who indeed is interceding for us." **Romans 8: 33-34.**

There is no longer any condemnation that can stand before God. So, you can no longer live with the consequences of sin. *"There is therefore now no condemnation for those who are in Christ Jesus."* **Romans 8: 1**

The bonds and consequences of the sins and covenants of your ancestors and blood relatives can no longer affect you and your descendants.

It is no longer acceptable for you to suffer the consequences of a sin, or a covenant made by your parents and ancestors. You can no longer live all that is recur- rent in your life as evil, poverty, disease because it has been transmitted by blood or family. It is your responsibility to claim it and live it!

It is no longer acceptable for you to suffer the implications. You can no longer live all that is recurrent in your life as evil, poverty, disease because it was transmitted by blood. You will no longer live the consequences of what the forefathers did; it is up to you to proclaim it and claim it because the enemy has no right to make you live it.

It is your responsibility to claim it and live it!

Refuse to live the consequences of the acts of your parents and ancestors as it is written, "In those days they shall no longer say: *"The fathers have eaten sour grapes, and the children's teeth are set on edge.' But everyone shall die for his own iniquity. Each man who eats sour grapes, his teeth shall be set on edge."* **Jeremiah 31: 29 - 30**

Forgiveness stops the cycle of consequences, curses, illnesses, barrenness, poverty, and introduces a new season. Your father's illness, your parents' divorce, your family's immorality no longer have a basis to affect you.

Forgiveness introduces a new season of blessing for you.

"The Lord passed before him and proclaimed, "The Lord, the Lord, a God merciful and gracious, slow to anger, and abounding in steadfast love and faithfulness, keeping steadfast love for thousands, forgiving iniquity and transgression and sin, but who will by no means clear the guilty, visiting the iniquity of the fathers on the children and the children's children, to the third and the fourth generation." **Exodus 34: 6 - 7**

Plead the blood of the Lamb in cases of guilt and condemnation. It works!

For no accusation, no condemnation, no sin, and its consequences can stand against the blood of the Lamb. This one speaks louder than any other argument.

"But you have come to Mount Zion and to the city of the living God, the heavenly Jerusalem, and to innumerable angels in festal gathering, and to the assembly of the first-born who are enrolled in heaven, and to God, the judge of all, and to the spirits of the righteous made perfect, and to Jesus, the mediator of a new covenant, and to the sprinkled blood that speaks a better word than the blood of Abel." **Hebrews 12: 22 - 24**

The word of our testimony

*"And they have conquered him by **the blood of the Lamb** and by the **word of their testimony**, for they loved **not their lives even unto death.**"* **Revelation 12: 11**

There is no need to remind ourselves of the power of witnessing in the life of a Christian, or better still in the process of victory.

We need to remember that we have first the inner witness of the Spirit who bears witness to our spirit that we are children of God.

"The Spirit himself bears witness with our spirit that we are children of God," **Romans 8: 16.**

This passage enshrines the victory over the guilt of the enemy which he imposes on our hearts so that we may always consider ourselves sinners. He who condemns himself cannot defeat the enemy, for accusation is one of his effective weapons against sinners and Christians.

"And I heard a loud voice in heaven, saying, "Now the salvation and the power and the kingdom of our God and the authority of his Christ have come, for the accuser of our brothers has been thrown down, who accuses them day and night before our God." **Revelation 12: 10**

Our enemy is a full-time accuser, so don't give him an opportunity to weaken you and especially to make you feel guilty. He who feels guilty is a prisoner and therefore not free; he will be defeated by his own testimony.

Then there is the testimony of the word of God, what we receive from the word, the message of revelation that consecrates the victory of God over the enemy in all its forms. The testimony of the word is so powerful that nothing can stand. We bear witness to what we have seen, heard, and touched in relation to God. The testimony is special in that it is a lived reality, what God has already done in our lives.

"But you will receive power when the Holy Spirit has come upon you, and you will be my witnesses in Jerusalem and in all Judea and Samaria, and to the end of the earth." **Acts 1: 8**

We have received the Holy Spirit to be witnesses everywhere, the testimony we proclaim, the death and resurrection of Jesus-Christ is the key to our testimony on earth and this is what guarantees us victory against the enemy because he does not want us to be witnesses of what we have heard, what we have seen with our eyes, what we have contemplated and what our hands have touched concerning the word of life according to what is written in

1 John 1: 1 - 3.[47]

- We are witnesses of the resurrection (**Acts 2: 23 - 24**[48]).
- We are witnesses of what God has done and is doing, which we know (**Isaiah 43: 10**[49])
- We are witnesses of the good news (**Acts 8: 4**[50])
- We are witnesses to the life of Jesus (**1 John 1: 1 - 3**)

---

47. **1 John 1 : 1 - 3** *"That which was from the beginning, which we have heard, which we have seen with our eyes, which we looked upon and have touched with our hands, concerning the word of life— the life was made manifest, and we have seen it, and testify to it and proclaim to you the eternal life, which was with the Father and was made manifest to us"*

48. **Acts 2: 23 - 24** *"this Jesus, delivered up according to the definite plan and foreknowledge of God, you crucified and killed by the hands of lawless men. God raised him up, loosing the pangs of death, because it was not possible for him to be held by it."*

49. **Isaiah 43: 10** *"You are my witnesses," declares the Lord, "and my servant whom I have chosen, that you may know and believe me and understand that I am he. Before me no god was formed, nor shall there be any after me."*

50. **Acts 8: 4** *"Now those who were scattered went about preaching the word."*

- We are witnesses of eternal life.
- We are witnesses of the light.
- We are witnesses to confess the name of Jesus-Christ **(Matthew 10: 32 - 33[51], Mark 8: 38[52])**
- We are witnesses that Jesus-Christ is the Son of God (**1 John 4: 15[53]**)

In the end, it is essential to proclaim and declare these words of testimony. There is a power attached to it every time our mouths proclaim it. Declare eternal life, light, good news, and the name of Jesus. Let all that is testimony in your heart and mind never be silent. Give voice to the inner testimony; you will see the victory! The enemy does not want to hear these words of testimony that finish him.

---

51. **Matthew 10: 32-33** *"So everyone who acknowledges me before men, I also will acknowledge before my Father who is in heaven, but whoever denies me before men, I also will deny before my Father who is in heaven."*

52. **Mark 8: 38** *"For whoever is ashamed of me and of my words in this adulterous and sinful generation, of him will the Son of Man also be ashamed when he comes in the glory of his Father with the holy angels."*

53. **1 John 4: 15** *"Whoever confesses that Jesus is the Son of God, God abides in him, and he in God."*

The sacrifice of life, giving one's life and dying for God.

"For they loved not their lives even unto death."

How is the sacrifice of life a victory against our enemy? Of course, Jesus himself had already answered this question. His life is an answer to this question. He defeated the devil because he did not refuse to keep his life, he sacrificed himself by giving himself to the death of the cross.

"Then Jesus told his disciples, "If anyone would come after me, let him deny himself and take up his cross and follow me. For whoever would save his life will lose it, but whoever loses his life for my sake will find it." **Matthew 16: 24 - 25.**

No one can defeat the devil if he is not prepared to die for the cause of Jesus-Christ. The first Christians showed this gift to the point of being for the most part martyrs and especially to take the risk of prison, whips ...

It is those who have this attitude, like Daniel and his companions, Stephen stoned to death, Peter crucified upside down, Paul beheaded, who defeated the enemy because the enemy could not prevent them from bearing witness even at the risk of their lives. And today we are the beneficiaries of the sacrifices of the first martyrs of the Church. We must remember that the word martyr comes from the Greek and means a witness.

One cannot be a witness without being ready to die for the cause of Christ.

It must also be said that the power of our witness has been overshadowed by our love of life; we no longer take risks for the cause of the Kingdom of God. Our messages tend more towards enjoying life and not losing it, and that is why the enemy is often gaining ground not only in our lives but also in our churches.

Are we, in turn, willing to sacrifice our lives for the cause of Christ?

There is victory against the enemy in the sacrifice of life and the absence of the fear of death. Could we say like Paul, Christ is my life, and death is my gain?

"For to me to live is Christ, and to die is gain." **Philippians 1: 21**

APPLICATION

1. I become a prayerful advocate.
2. I learn to use the argument of the blood of the Lamb.

CHAPTER 7

SPEAKING IN TONGUES TO BUILD AND STRENGTHEN YOUR DESTINY

I would be incomplete if I did not speak of this precious gift, which the Holy Spirit gives us as an instrument to build our destiny and also as an effective weapon for prayer and intercession. As it is called, it is the gift of speaking in tongues or otherwise of words in unknown languages.

I don't pretend to talk about all that speaking in tongues is, but I would simply like to highlight the fact that speaking in tongues builds your destiny and creates new situations in your life. I would recommend Kenneth Hagin's book, "Tongues: Beyond the Upper Room," which is a comprehensive masterpiece on this issue, and I have drawn on it a lot. I'll just emphasize here the aspect of the connection with the impact of words in our lives.

It is true that it is the gift or manifestation of the Spirit that we only see in the New Testament. The Old Testament does not speak of it at all, which has led many to give it less importance or to take it as an accessory gift compared to the others.

We can either live it or not yet. I still remember the first time I was baptized in the Holy Spirit with evidence of speaking in tongues, it was the same day I gave my life to Jesus-Christ on November 27, 1993. For some it happened later and for others even in the years after, It must be said that it also depends on who preached the

Gospel to you. Did he give you the opportunity to receive the baptism of the Holy Spirit as well, to be filled with the Holy Spirit?

It may also be that you have never heard of the baptism of the Holy Spirit with the evidence of speaking in tongues because you have been presented as if the day you received or accepted Jesus-Christ, you also received the Holy Spirit, and it is all the Holy Spirit that you must receive. I have heard these teachings before!

The baptism of the Holy Spirit is an experience that is different from salvation.

As we read through the Bible, it is indeed another experience apart from salvation (you have received the Holy Spirit at the same time), it is the baptism or the fullness of the Holy Spirit.

"I baptize you with water for repentance, but he who is coming after me is mightier than I, whose sandals I am not worthy to carry. He will baptize you with the Holy Spirit and fire." **Matthew 3: 11**

John the Baptist is the first to speak of the baptism of the Holy Spirit and fire in relation to the mission of Jesus-Christ. It is clear that like the other baptisms, this one too is after repentance and salvation. This prophecy of John the Baptist in **Matthew 3: 11** was fulfilled on the day of Pentecost when those who had already believed in him awaited the fulfillment of the promise of baptism or fullness.

John the Baptist therefore presents the baptism of the Holy Spirit as an act that will follow faith. It is impossible to receive this baptism without having received the one who baptizes you with the Holy Spirit and fire. The apostles of Jesus-Christ, after his ascension, should wait for the fullness in the upper room in Jerusalem.

"for John baptized with water, but you will be baptized with the Holy Spirit not many days from now." So when they had come together, they asked him, "Lord, will you at this time restore the kingdom to Israel?" He said to them, "It is not for you to know times or seasons that the Father has fixed by his own authority. But you will receive power when the Holy Spirit has come upon you, and you will be my witnesses in Jerusalem and in all Judea and Samaria, and to the end of the earth." **Acts 1: 5 - 8**

The apostles did not receive the baptism of the Holy Spirit or the fullness of the Holy Spirit on the same day they believed. It was later, at Pentecost, that they experienced it and began to speak in other tongues.

Peter presents the baptism of the Holy Spirit as subsequent to salvation.

"And Peter said to them, "Repent and be baptized every one of you in the name of Jesus-Christ for the forgiveness of your sins, and you will receive the gift of the Holy Spirit. For the promise is for you and for your children and for all who are far off, everyone whom the Lord our God calls to himself." **Acts 2: 38 - 39**

Peter, whom I call the apostle of the birth of the Church, also presents things in the same way. Baptism is very different from the experience of salvation and therefore we need this baptism for our walk and especially our ministry as Christians. It is the key to a powerful witness in the mission to fulfil the supreme command to go and make disciples of all nations.

So, when the apostles heard that Philip had preached in Samaria where the disciples had received the word, Peter and John were sent to lay hands on them to receive the Holy Spirit. It is true that it is not clear that they spoke in other languages from **Acts 8: 5 - 17**[54].

---

54. **Acts 8: 5-17** *"Philip went down to the city of Samaria and proclaimed to them the Christ. And the crowds with one accord paid attention to what was being said by Philip, when they heard him and saw the signs that he did. For unclean spirits, crying out with a loud voice, came out of many who had them, and many who were paralyzed or lame were healed. So there was much joy in that city. But there was a*

But I believe with Dr. Kenneth Hagin[55] that if Simon did not have the sign that they had received the Holy Spirit, namely by speaking in tongues, he would not have asked Peter and John to give him the power to communicate the Holy Spirit for a price. A student of church history knows that the church fathers agree that the believers in Samaria had spoken in tongues[56]. There was indeed evidence that Simon and the Bible commentators said that the believers in Samaria were indeed filled with this evidence. So, we need to know that at that very

---

man named Simon, who had previously practiced magic in the city and amazed the people of Samaria, saying that he himself was somebody great. They all paid attention to him, from the least to the greatest, saying, "This man is the power of God that is called Great." And they paid attention to him because for a long time he had amazed them with his magic. But when they believed Philip as he preached good news about the kingdom of God and the name of Jesus-Christ, they were baptized, both men and women. Even Simon himself believed, and after being baptized he continued with Philip. And seeing signs and great miracles performed, he was amazed. Now when the apostles at Jerusalem heard that Samaria had received the word of God, they sent to them Peter and John, who came down and prayed for them that they might receive the Holy Spirit, for he had not yet fallen on any of them, but they had only been baptized in the name of the Lord Jesus. Then they laid their hands on them and they received the Holy Spirit."

55. Kenneth Hagin, Tongues: beyond the upper room, Faith Library Publications, 2007, p.35

56. Kenneth Hagin, Tongues: beyond the upper room, Faith Library Publications, 2007, p.35.

moment it was the outward sign that made observers, including the apostles, say that a person on whom they had just laid hands had been filled with the Holy Spirit.

Paul speaks of the baptism of the Holy Spirit as being subsequent to salvation.

He, whom I call the Apostle of the life of the Church or of the management of the Church, first experienced salvation on the road to Damascus where he met Jesus in a miraculous way.

"Now as he went on his way, he approached Damascus, and suddenly a light from heaven shone around him. And falling to the ground, he heard a voice saying to him, "Saul, Saul, why are you persecuting me?" And he said, "Who are you, Lord?" And he said, "I am Jesus, whom you are persecuting. But rise and enter the city, and you will be told what you are to do." **Acts 9: 3 - 6**

So, he was saved, as he would explain himself later in Jerusalem in Acts 22[57].

---

57. **Acts 22: 3-11,18** *"I am a Jew, born in Tarsus in Cilicia, but brought up in this city, educated at the feet of Gamaliel according to the strict manner of the law of our fathers, being zealous for God as all of you are this day. I persecuted this Way to the death, binding and delivering to prison both men and women, as the high priest and the whole*

Then as he could no longer see, and especially as he had to continue to bear witness to Jesus-Christ as his instrument, he needed a disciple, better Ananias, not only to recover his sight but also to be filled with the Holy Spirit. Again, Paul had already been chosen as an instrument before Ananias laid hands on him for the filling of the Holy Spirit.

The question remains, did he speak in tongues as evidence of this filling?

And how do we know?

Especially since we do not see clearly here that he had just spoken in other tongues. We assume it from the

---

council of elders can bear me witness. From them I received letters to the brothers, and I journeyed toward Damascus to take those also who were there and bring them in bonds to Jerusalem to be punished. "As I was on my way and drew near to Damascus, about noon a great light from heaven suddenly shone around me. And I fell to the ground and heard a voice saying to me, 'Saul, Saul, why are you persecuting me?' And I answered, 'Who are you, Lord?' And he said to me, 'I am Jesus of Nazareth, whom you are persecuting.' Now those who were with me saw the light but did not understand the voice of the one who was speaking to me. And I said, 'What shall I do, Lord?' And the Lord said to me, 'Rise, and go into Damascus, and there you will be told all that is appointed for you to do.' And since I could not see because of the brightness of that light, I was led by the hand by those who were with me, and came into Damascus. and saw him saying to me, 'Make haste and get out of Jerusalem quickly, because they will not accept your testimony about me."

moment Ananias laid his hands on him. In other words, whenever we see in the Acts of the Apostles talking about the fullness of the Holy Spirit or his Baptism, we must discern that they had just spoken in tongues because that was the only way to know at that time that believers were being filled or baptized with the Holy Spirit. That was the manifestation and the outward sign. They did not question it; it was so clear that they did not need to specify it.

There is not enough time to talk about Paul's experience with the disciples of John the Baptist about the baptism of the Holy Spirit. This story is interesting in that we see how Paul is following exactly the pattern of the other Apostles like Peter and John in administering the baptism of the Holy Spirit, he is asking the same questions as Peter, the other apostles and disciples in Acts.

"And he said to them, "Did you receive the Holy Spirit when you believed?" And they said, "No, we have not even heard that there is a Holy Spirit." And Paul said, "John baptized with the baptism of repentance, telling the people to believe in the one who was to come after him, that is, Jesus." On hearing this, they were baptized in the name of the Lord Jesus. ***And when Paul had laid his hands on them, the Holy Spirit came on them, and they began speaking in tongues and prophesying.*** *There were about twelve men in all."* **Acts 19: 2,4 - 7**

It is evident here that Paul himself applied the process of his own experience as well as that of the church fathers like Peter and John to pray for the baptism of the Holy Spirit. He laid hands on the disciples, and they began to speak in tongues and prophesy. This is exactly what he and other believers of the time had experienced. This is the pattern left by the early fathers and disciples who experienced the baptism or filling of the Holy Spirit with the outward sign of speaking in tongues.

Paul also followed his own experience of how he had been baptized in the Holy Spirit.

How did the believers in Acts know that they were filled with the Holy Spirit?

This is an interesting question in that its answer will help us to recognize the baptism, and for this we must go back to the first experience in Acts 2. It is worth recalling that Jesus had recommended that they wait in Jerusalem for the baptism of the Holy Spirit, and when it came upon them, they began to speak in other tongues, among other manifestations of that day. The first sign of baptism they identified was hearing speaking in tongues. They linked this to the baptism and the miracle also spoken of in **Mark 16: 17.**

The apostles and disciples identified speaking in tongues as a sign or evidence of baptism or the filling of the Holy Spirit. Wherever they saw this sign, it followed the laying on of hands for believers to receive baptism or the full- ness. I have no doubt that for the early church fathers and disciples of the time when we look at their records, speaking in tongues was evidence of the baptism or filling of the Holy Spirit. It was what they saw God do, it was the pattern, and it is documented by the experiences recorded in Luke.

One of the weaknesses of the Church in our time is that we do not want to follow the model of the early fathers, we accommodate ourselves to justify the weakness of our witness, the lack of power of our generation.

If the apostles had this experience for their testimony and we avoid it, we will not be able to manifest the power that they demonstrated. If they were baptized in the Holy Spirit with evidence of speaking in tongues, we should also follow in their footsteps.

132

Speaking in tongues, one of the signs of belief and salvation.

Speaking in tongues is also an external sign that the one who is baptized in it, believes in God, and is granted this gift by the Holy Spirit. Moreover, it is a promise that was made to believers only and mainly to enable them to have a powerful testimony. So, when we go through the scriptures, we will see that only those who believed benefited from it in the book of Acts.

No salvation, no speaking in tongues when we read Acts 2, 8, 9, 10 and 19. Only those who believed, spoke in tongues.

"In him you also, when you heard the word of truth, the gospel of your salvation, and believed in him, were sealed with the promised Holy Spirit, who is the guarantee of our inheritance until we acquire possession of it, to the praise of his glory." **Ephesians 1: 13-14**

As such, we can also say that speaking in tongues is a sign of the Holy Spirit, a pledge of our salvation, a seal of our God. We can deduce that speaking in tongues is the evidence of the baptism of the Holy Spirit and is therefore the outward sign that we have the Holy Spirit within us. For it is given to those who have believed to guarantee them redemption by this seal of the Spirit.

It is true that if someone has the Holy Spirit in him, we have no other signs to know it, but with the speaking in tongues, we can safely say that the one who speaks in tongues, has been baptized with the Holy Spirit. This only happens in Christians.

What is the point of speaking in an unknown or new language?

The first evangelist who speaks of speaking in tongues is Mark, who presents it as one of the five miraculous signs that accompany those who believe in Jesus-Christ. Here, it is a miracle and, as such, it is supernatural.

If you speak in tongues, you have already seen a miracle or witnessed a supernatural thing in your life. I respect this miracle that God has granted me.

"And these signs will accompany those who believe: in my name they will cast out demons; they will speak in new tongues; they will pick up serpents with their hands; and if they drink any deadly poison, it will not hurt them; they will lay their hands on the sick, and they will recover." **Mark 16: 17 - 18**

134
Speaking in tongues is a means of encrypted communication.

Generally speaking, a language is a means of communication to get along or to transmit a message. As such, speaking in tongues remains primarily a means of communication between the speaker and the recipient. The speaker is addressing the receiver, and the receiver understands him or her very well. When we speak in tongues, we have an interlocutor who understands us very well in what we say.

When you speak in tongues, God understands you perfectly well; he is even the only one who understands you because you are telling him mysteries.

So, if we speak in tongues, the people around us do not understand it because they are not the ones who should understand it. So, it is a coded or encrypted message for everyone else; only the recipient can process it.

"For one who speaks in a tongue speaks not to men but to God; for no one understands him, but he utters mysteries in the Spirit." **1 Corinthians 14: 2**

"For one who speaks in an unknown tongue does not speak to people but to God; for no one understands him or catches his meaning, but by the Spirit he speaks mysteries [secret truths, hidden things]." **1 Corinthians 14: 2 AMP.**

This message does not need to be interpreted for men because they are not the recipients. It is the recipient who knows how to decrypt the message addressed to him.

God gives it to me to communicate with him, to tell him mysteries. You just hear a word that is repeated, so it's like a binary language where you only have 01 or 00 numbers in a row, but it can be a whole message from the system. Only a processor can successfully process the code, interpret, or respond to the command.

I like the Sower Bible version of the verse.

"He that speaketh in an unknown tongue speaketh unto God, and not unto men: no man understandeth the mysterious words which he speaketh by inspiration of the Spirit"

He who speaks in tongues speaks mysterious words under the inspiration of the Holy Spirit. He is the one who knows the things of God and its depths according to **1 Corinthians 2: 10**[58].

He knows exactly what to say to God. Prayers made in tongues never miss their target; the Holy Spirit who

---

58 **1 Corinthians 2: 10 AMP** *"For God has unveiled them and revealed them to us through the [Holy] Spirit; for the Spirit searches all things [diligently], even [sounding and measuring] the [profound] depths of God [the divine counsels and things far beyond human understanding]"*.

inspires them knows exactly what our needs are and what to say. Also, the Holy Spirit knows God's thoughts and plans; he helps us to pray according to God's mind or according to his plans.

Since we pray according to the Spirit or under the inspiration of the Holy Spirit, we know how to say exactly the right thing because we have the help of the Holy Spirit who knows the hidden plans and thoughts of God. So, we have a double advantage here, we communicate with God with an encrypted language, and we know exactly what God's plans and thoughts are in our prayer in tongues.

Just imagine once what the impact of such communication or prayer can be. We could not have a better communication system and technology.

I pray in tongues because only God understands me and no one else can hear the secrets I tell God. Also, I know exactly what to ask for because I have the help of the Spirit who knows the hidden plans and thoughts of God.

I also believe that God wanted us to have a communication system that even the enemy cannot decipher so that he cannot intercept and organize attacks on us or prevent certain things. What the enemy does not know, he does not know how to counteract. When he intercepts our prayers, he may seek to thwart them. When he hears, he can fight it, he can set up strategies to steal, destroy...

As the enemy cannot access our spirit, the things that are there are not accessible to him, he will only have to wait to hear us say them so that he can organize his attack.

Some things are hidden so that the unauthorized cannot access them.

Expressing yourself in tongues has impact and power.

When we read Paul's letter to the Corinthians, in which he talks about speaking in tongues and draws a parallel with prophecy and the interpretation of tongues, it is important to mention that this letter is addressed in a particular context: it is a church where not only immorality reigned but also disorder. So, Paul is going to reframe many things. But as far as the spiritual gifts are concerned, including speaking in tongues, they were operational, far from preventing their exercise; he wanted to frame them; that is why sometimes you have the impression that he is discouraging speaking in tongues in the absence of interpretation. Without con- text, it will be difficult to understand Paul's positions. Some people have understood that to speak in tongues in the church, you need to have interpretation.

"I thank God that I speak in tongues more than all of you."
1 Corinthians 14: 18.

What an observation! Paul is speaking the truth and glorifies God for it. He had time to see the Corinthians certainly speaking in tongues in the church, and he observed that he spoke much more than they did. He did so because he knew the importance, value, and power of it. In addition to the other extracts in this epistle, he devotes a whole chapter to it (14).

If Paul's life, especially his prayer life, has had such an impact, it is also because he gave a place to prayer in tongues. He also expresses this when he tells the recipients that he wants them all to speak in tongues better than they prophesy.

"What am I to do? I will pray with my spirit, but I will pray with my mind also; I will sing praise with my spirit, but I will sing with my mind also." **1 Corinthians 14: 5**

He wanted the Corinthians to have the same impact as he did, a prayer life as powerful as his.

So, in the comparison between speaking in tongues and prophecy, we just need to understand that Paul wanted his recipients to be edified themselves, better still, to edify the church. This is the fundamental difference.

He who speaks in tongues edifies himself, whereas he who prophesies or interprets edifies the church.

Paul does not discourage anyone from building up or edifying himself.

He who speaks in tongues prays more than he who prays in understanding.

Again, if we take the context of church edification out of the picture, we may think that Paul is discouraging praying in tongues in the church when he is emphasizing edification in the church as one of the purposes of spiritual gifts. Nevertheless, he had already established that he who speaks in tongues speaks to God, he speaks mysteries under the inspiration of the Holy Spirit. It is clear that he who prays under the inspiration of the Spirit with the depths of God, his prayer in terms of effectiveness is effective. He prays according to the plans and thoughts of God with the help of the Spirit who knows the depths of God.

If I pray in understanding, I need my head, mouth and reason too. Whereas when I pray in tongue, I just need my mouth, so the one who prays in tongue gets less tired than the one who prays in understanding only, he will end up repeating the same words at some point.

Since I decided to pray in tongues, my prayer life is growing not only in quality but also in time spent in God's presence. I can pray for hours without getting tired, but for the same timing, it takes a lot of discipline to pray in intelligence.

Praying in tongue improves your prayer life significantly more than praying with understanding. I pray in tongue and in mind, but I spend much more time praying in tongue than in mind. Two-thirds of my prayer life is spent praying in tongues and I can see the difference from when I prayed much more in understanding than in tongue.

However, in the church we need to pray with our minds so that others can not only be edified but also be able to say amen to our prayer.

Prayer in tongues builds your destiny.

"The one who speaks in a tongue builds up himself, but the one who prophesies builds up the church." **1 Corinthians 14: 4 ESV.**

"One who speaks in a tongue edifies himself; but one who prophesies edifies the church [promotes growth in spiritual wisdom, devotion, holiness, and joy]." **1 Corinthians 14: 4 AMP.**

"Anyone who speaks in a different language only helps himself. But a person who speaks a message from God helps the believers in the church to become strong." **1 Corinthians 14: 4 EASY.**

"He that speaketh in an unknown tongue edifieth himself; but he that prophesieth edifieth the church." **1 Corinthians 14: 4 KJV.**

Nevertheless, those who speak in tongues are also doing very beneficial work for their spiritual life, that of building themselves up, strengthening themselves.

Paul establishes two systems of building or edification, one for his own destiny through speaking in tongues and the other for the church through prophecy or interpretation of tongues.

The words that one speaks in tongues are like bricks of a building. Every moment that you spend speaking, something is being, built in your life. It is these words that are bricks. They have such a beneficial or profitable effect on our lives that anyone who understands the principle should not refrain from speaking in tongues. Words have a meaning or a constructive capacity in our life.

If simple words have a life-giving or death-giving capacity, how can they not be the words that are inspired by the Holy Spirit? For it is in spirit that we speak in tongues, we speak things that only the Spirit understands.

- The words of prayer in tongues are more powerful than the words of prayer with understanding.

- The words of prayer in tongues come from the Spirit, they are inspired by Him to have constructive, beneficial, and profitable effects on our spiritual life.

- The words in prayer in tongues are addressed to God but with a boomerang effect on us because they come back with the power of our edification, construction, strengthening.

- Prayers in tongues are for our good, our profit, and our benefit.

- Words in tongues forge and build a destiny, they are materials for the construction or building of our destiny.

When I pray in spirit (in tongue) I am building myself up, and so you know what you need to do to have an abundant and powerful spiritual life, it is simple: you need to edify, build, and construct using the materials that the words spoken in tongue are.

He who speaks in tongues builds his destiny with solid materials.

He who speaks in tongues creates new situations in his spiritual environment.

To speak in tongues continuously is to build one's destiny continuously.

APPLICATION

1. I pray in tongues much more than I pray with understanding in my personal prayer life.

2. I introduce speaking in tongues into my prayer system.

CHAPTER 8

THE WORDS THAT IMPACT YOUR DESTINY AND THAT OF YOUR OFFSPRING

Reading the biographies of Abraham, Isaac, and Jacob teaches us and gives us very important principles about blessings, and their transmissibility to one's posterity or offspring. From the outset, we can say that the blessing of one's offspring is the greatest inheritance that you can leave to your descendants. We will therefore review the principles on the transmissibility of the blessings and promises that God has given us.

The transmissibility of blessings and promises.

First of all, it should be pointed out that every great and good blessing is transgenerational and as such, it is transmissible to anyone. It is therefore difficult for God to give you a blessing and for it to be limited to yourself. Let us try to review the history of our patriarchs.

We must remember that God, presenting himself to Moses, identified himself as the God of his father Abraham, Isaac, and Jacob[59]. And later, Jesus-Christ, speaking of God as the one of the livings, also invoked him as the God of Abraham, Isaac, and Jacob again[60].

---

59. **Exodus 3: 6** *"And he said, "I am the God of your father, the God of Abraham, the God of Isaac, and the God of Jacob." And Moses hid his face, for he was afraid to look at God."*

60. **Matthew 22: 31-32** *"And as for the resurrection of the dead, have*

To this end, the minimum level or generation to which God can impart a blessing is the third generation. Better still, it is to your grandchildren that you can judge the transmissibility of your inheritance or blessings. Otherwise, a promise, blessing, or inheritance can go to the thousandth generation.

"You shall not bow down to them or serve them, for I the Lord your God am a jealous God, visiting the iniquity of the fathers on the children to the third and the fourth generation of those who hate me, but showing steadfast love to thousands of those who love me and keep my commandments." **Exodus 20: 5 - 6**

Some principles on the transmissibility of blessings and promises.

- It is God who ensures the transmissibility of a blessing from father to son or to offspring.
- When God blesses you, he has also blessed your offspring to the thousandth generation.
- Your father's promises are automatically your promises too unless a curse is pronounced.
- The goodness of God is also transmissible to

---

you not read what was said to you by God: 'I am the God of Abraham, and the God of Isaac, and the God of Jacob'? He is not God of the dead, but of the living."

future generations.[61]

- In the same way that God passes on the blessing, he can also pass on the curse, but only to the fourth generation. See **Exodus 34: 6 - 7**

- Your father's blessing is a right. If you do not live it, it is your right to claim it. You will live it unless there is a sin that has come in between. Your faith in Jesus-Christ is the best guarantee for your heirs. He has blessed us with all kinds of blessings in heavenly places, and these are passed on to your children by right. If God has shown us his love through Jesus-Christ, this is also a guarantee for our children. I understand why Paul and Silas said to the jailer: *"And they said, "Believe in the Lord Jesus, and you will be saved, you and your household."*[62]

- When God blesses you, he does it also for your seed. It is the only way for him to guarantee

---

61. **Exodus 34 : 6-7** *"The Lord passed before him and proclaimed, "The Lord , the Lord , a God merciful and gracious, slow to anger, and abounding in steadfast love and faithfulness, keeping steadfast love for thousands, forgiving iniquity and transgression and sin, but who will by no means clear the guilty, visiting the iniquity of the fathers on the children and the children's children, to the third and the fourth generation."*

62. **Acts 16: 31** *"And they said, "Believe in the Lord Jesus, and you will be saved, you and your household."*

its transmissibility from generation to generation.

Prepare the destiny of your children by the words of your mouth.

"And prepare for me delicious food, such as I love, and bring it to me so that I may eat, that my soul may bless you before I die." Rebekah said to her son Jacob, "I heard your father speak to your brother Esau, 'Bring me game and prepare for me delicious food, that I may eat it and bless you before the Lord before I die.' So he came near and kissed him. And Isaac smelled the smell of his garments and blessed him and said, "See, the smell of my son is as the smell of a field that the Lord has blessed! May God give you of the dew of heaven and of the fatness of the earth and plenty of grain and wine. Let peoples serve you, and nations bow down to you. Be lord over your brothers and may your mother's sons bow down to you. Cursed be everyone who curses you, and blessed be everyone who blesses you!" **Genesis 27: 4,6 - 7,27 - 29**

In the matter of blessing, one's offspring, it is important to note that it is the responsibility of the father to precede the destiny of his children. The fathers in Israel knew that this was their responsibility to the point that there was a ceremonial on the occasion. Isaac will ask that a delicious dish be prepared for him to enhance the atmosphere in which the words of his mouth should be proclaimed. It is important to note that it was not God who asked Isaac to do this, but he wanted to do it as was customary. Rebekah knew that all the words Isaac was going to speak would come to pass. Isaac spoke the words over Jacob thinking he was doing it over Esau, but this did not prevent them from being fulfilled. The principle is that they are words that are fulfilled no matter what the circumstances or over whom they are spoken. Here are some principles that we can draw from these passages:

1. The words a father speaks over his children are so powerful, no matter the circumstances and conditions in which they are spoken.

2. It is the responsibility of every father to proceed with the blessing of his children. God is waiting for you to do them so that heaven and earth will witness them.

3. A father's blessings and curses are fulfilled because of the authority of the father and the power of any words spoken.

4. Every father must be aware of the power of his words on the destiny of his children so that he does not neglect what comes out of his mouth.

5. A father's words have as much power as prophe-

cies, for he is invested with this authority by God. He is the source of life for his child.

6. Jacob's cunning did not prevent the fulfillment of the blessing, and Isaac could not revoke the words spoken because they had already been established in the spiritual and invisible world. Isaac was seized with a great, violent emotion, and he said, *"Then Isaac trembled very violently and said, "Who was it then that hunted game and brought it to me, and I ate it all before you came, and I have blessed him? Yes, and he shall be blessed."* **Genesis 27: 33**.

This is how a father must know how to manage his heart; otherwise, it is poison that you can pronounce on your children because of what you expect from them. Should we have a heart like that of Christ who, despite what the world did to him, spoke words of forgiveness instead: "Father forgive them for they know not what they do."[63]

7. The father had better speak words of blessing over his offspring because your child's failure is also your failure. His success is your success too. This implies that with a father's heart and

---

63. Luke 23: 33 - 34 *"And when they came to the place that is called The Skull, there they crucified him, and the criminals, one on his right and one on his left. And Jesus said, "Father, forgive them, for they know not what they do." And they cast lots to divide his garments."*

love, you cannot subject your children or your offspring to curses. If a child fails, the father is somewhat responsible.

8. It should be noted that it was not God who asked Isaac to speak these words, but he did so as a father and guarantor of the transmissibility of the promises he himself had inherited from his father Abraham and those he had also received from God.

9. The father is the guarantor of the continuity of his promises to his children insofar as he is not the sole beneficiary. Abraham alone could not ensure the promised multitude or nations, there had to be Isaac, Ishmael and the other children of Keturah.

10. The words you speak about your children precede them in their future and mark out their destiny, you should be aware of this.

153

The words about your children or offspring always come true.

"Jacob called his sons together and said: My sons, I am Jacob, your father Israel. Come, gather around, as I tell your future." **Genesis 49: 1 - 2 CEV.**

"Then Jacob called for his sons and said, "Assemble yourselves [around me] that I may tell you what will happen to you and your descendants in the days to come. Gather together and hear, O sons of Jacob; And listen to Israel (Jacob) your father." **Genesis 49: 1 - 2 AMP.**

All the blessings spoken go up to verse 29, clearly it will be difficult to go through all these blessings and their fulfillment, but we will take a sample to see how they are all fulfilled.

Jacob gathered his children together to tell them what would happen in their future. There is no doubt that these words will be fulfilled in the future. The question is much more about the quality of the words. It should also be noted that some of the blessings or words have a relationship with the character and shortcomings of his children, their behaviors did affect the words that Jacob spoke about his children.

All these words come from the heart of Jacob with all the considerations and knowledge he had about his children.

God has given you the authority to affect the destiny of your children or offspring. The good news is, we have, and we are better than Jacob, for we have the Holy Spirit within us capable of inspiring us with the best blessings to pronounce on our children according to the depths we receive from God over their lives and future.

I will say it better than the commentator of the Bible Expliquée Commentaires[64] of the chapter 49 of Genesis says "the blessings Jacob gives to his twelve sons are difficult to understand; they are illuminated by the history of each of the tribes and, therefore, are like the style of prophecy. The two most developed blessings are for Judah and Joseph. Perhaps because Judah and Ephraim will form the nucleus of the future kingdoms of the South and North."

I really believe that these blessings are prophetic because they have been fulfilled as demonstrated by the later times in Jacob's family.

Let's just take verse 10 and following about Judah from whom Jesus-Christ came out to see the continuation of the fulfillment of this blessing in Judah's descendants.

---

64. Bible Expliquée Commentaires de Genèse 49, Editions de 2004.

"Judah, your brothers shall praise you; your hand shall be on the neck of your enemies; your father's sons shall bow down before you. Judah is a lion's cub; from the prey, my son, you have gone up. He stooped down; he crouched as a lion and as a lioness; who dares rouse him? The scepter shall not depart from Judah, nor the ruler's staff from between his feet, until tribute comes to him; and to him shall be the obedience of the peoples." **Genesis 49: 8 - 10**

There is no doubt that this blessing is linked to the true lion of the tribe of Judah, which had kingship. It is a blessing that travelled down to Jesus-Christ descending from this tribe through Joseph the husband of Mary according to **Matthew 1: 16**.[65]

"And one of the elders said to me, "Weep no more; behold, the Lion of the tribe of Judah, the Root of David, has conquered, so that he can open the scroll and its seven seals." **Revelation 5: 5**

Judah is the royal tribe, and it has given kings up to the King of kings who is the Lord Jesus-Christ.

Let us also look at the blessing of Joseph and its consequences in the future.

"Judah, your brothers shall praise you; your hand shall

---

65. **Matthew 1: 16** *"and Jacob the father of Joseph the husband of Mary, of whom Jesus was born, who is called Christ."*

be on the neck of your enemies; your father's sons shall bow down before you. "Joseph is a fruitful bough, a fruitful bough by a spring; his branches run over the wall. The archers bitterly attacked him, shot at him, and harassed him severely, yet his bow remained unmoved; his arms were made agile by the hands of the Mighty One of Jacob (from there is the Shepherd, the Stone of Israel), by the God of your father who will help you, by the Almighty who will bless you with blessings of heaven above, blessings of the deep that crouches beneath, blessings of the breasts and of the womb. The blessings of your father are mighty beyond the blessings of my parents, up to the bounties of the ever- lasting hills. May they be on the head of Joseph, and on the brow of him who was set apart from his brothers." **Gene- sis 49: 8,22 - 26**

To better understand this blessing, we should read 1 Chronicles 5:1, which gives a full explanation of the essence of the blessing in question.

" The sons of Reuben the firstborn of Israel (for he was the firstborn, but because he defiled his father's couch, his birthright was given to the sons of Joseph the son of Israel, so that he could not be enrolled as the oldest son; though Judah became strong among his brothers and a chief came from him, yet the birthright belonged to Joseph), the sons of Reuben, the firstborn of Israel: Hanoch, Pallu, Hezron, and Carmi." **1 Chronicles 5 : 1-3**

157
We are beneficiaries of the blessings of Abraham.

"And if you are Christ's, then you are Abraham's offspring, heirs according to promise." **Galatians 3: 29**

The blessings and promises of Abraham passed through Isaac and Jacob and finally through Jesus-Christ before reaching us. So, it is clear that the blessings Jacob pronounced on the 12 have reached us too. What about the curses on his children? They were transformed by Jesus-Christ because they could not stand in Jesus-Christ who became a curse according to the scriptures.

"Christ redeemed us from the curse of the law by becoming a curse for us—for it is written, "Cursed is everyone who is hanged on a tree"— so that in Christ Jesus the blessing of Abraham might come to the Gentiles, so that we might receive the promised Spirit through faith." **Galatians 3: 13 - 14**

Both blessings and curses were passed on but only Jesus-Christ transformed the curses because they could not pass through him to us. There is no justification for us to experience this, but we can experience all the blessings and promises of Abraham, Isaac and Jacob. Let us see how we can be beneficiaries of the blessings and promises of 12 spoken by Jacob in **Genesis 49**.

1. **Reuben**[66]: that you have superiority in strength and dignity, that you benefit from vigor and my power in life! you are the result of vigor and power! you are the first fruits of vigor. You surpass others in strength and power!

   This is the blessing you can pronounce on the elders.

2. **Simeon**[67]: Thou shalt not associate with the violent and the angry! Thou shalt not be in the company of those who meditate to do evil. Anger is cursed from your life; it will leave you and never linger in your life. You shall not take part in the deliberations of the wicked or in plots to do evil, to kill and to destroy the property and wealth of others.

3. **Levi**[68]: Thou shalt not associate with the violent and the angry! Thou shalt not be in the company

---

66. **Genesis 49: 3** *"Reuben, you are my firstborn, my might, and the firstfruits of my strength, preeminent in dignity and preeminent in power."*

67. **Genesis 49: 5-7** *"Simeon and Levi are brothers; weapons of violence are their swords. Let my soul come not into their council; O my glory, be not joined to their company. For in their anger, they killed men, and in their willfulness they hamstrung oxen."*

68. **See also Genesis 49: 5-7.**

of those who meditate to do evil. Anger is cursed from your life; it shall leave you and never linger in your life. You shall not take part in the deliberations of the wicked or in plots to do evil, to kill or to destroy the property and wealth of others.

4. **Judah**[69]: Let men pay homage to you, let them sing your praises, you will bend the neck of your enemies, you have the superiority over your enemies; the spirit of royalty is with you and you will win all your battles, power is your portion and scepter will not depart from you; you have abundance of joy and strength for your growth, abundance of wine and milk to guarantee your joy.

---

69. **Genesis 49: 8 - 12** *"Judah, your brothers shall praise you; your hand shall be on the neck of your enemies; your father's sons shall bow down before you. Judah is a lion's cub; from the prey, my son, you have gone up. He stooped down; he crouched as a lion and as a lioness; who dares rouse him? The scepter shall not depart from Judah, nor the ruler's staff from between his feet, until tribute comes to him; and to him shall be the obedience of the peoples. Binding his foal to the vine and his donkey's colt to the choice vine, he has washed his garments in wine and his vesture in the blood of grapes. His eyes are darker than wine, and his teeth whiter than milk."*

5. **Zebulun**[70]: May you have control and possession of the sea and land borders! May you have control of foreign trade, import and export. May you master the fishing of the seas, oceans, rivers, and the fish trade in import and export. May you have mastery over the riches of the waters and dominion over the spirits of the waters!

6. **Issakar**[71]: vigor in breeding and in mastering the pens; the robustness of the donkey (confidence because it does only what is asked of it, wide vision, fine hearing, strong hooves that do not need to be shod), it will place its trust always in God without doing anything of itself. May God use you as a donkey for His praise and message of good news to the world, an instrument to carry the message and praise of God. May you have the humility of a donkey so that Jesus-Christ may use you to announce his salvation to the world and proclaim the Kingdom of God as it is written in **Matthew 21: 1-3** *"Now when they drew near to Jerusalem and came to Bethphage, to the Mount of*

---

70. **Genesis 49: 13** *"Zebulun shall dwell at the shore of the sea; he shall become a haven for ships, and his border shall be at Sidon."*

71. **Genesis 49: 14 - 15** *"Issachar is a strong donkey, crouching between the sheepfolds. He saw that a resting place was good, and that the land was pleasant, so he bowed his shoulder to bear, and became a servant at forced labor."*

Olives, then Jesus sent two disciples, saying to them, "Go into the village in front of you, and immediately you will find a donkey tied, and a colt with her. Untie them and bring them to me. If anyone says anything to you, you shall say, 'The Lord needs them,' and he will send them at once.

7. **Dan**[72]: Let the leadership and authority of the judge be upon you, let you be the governor of many and of your people! Let you be a formidable enemy to adversaries and overthrow them by attacking them with their strength. May you be the one who brings deliverance for his people!

8. **Gad**[73]: he knows how to defend himself when he is attacked and pursues his enemies. May you counterattack your enemies! May you not be content to defend yourself, you are an attacker, may you pursue your enemies!

9. **Asher**[74]: Let you be the provider of the royal court with royal food and dishes! Let you be the servant of kings and have access to all levels of

---

72. **Genesis 49: 16 - 17** *"Dan shall judge his people as one of the tribes of Israel. Dan shall be a serpent in the way, a viper by the path, that bites the horse's heels so that his rider falls backward."*

73. **Genesis 49: 19** *"Raiders shall raid Gad, but he shall raid at their heels."*

74. **Genesis 49: 20** *"Asher's food shall be rich, and he shall yield royal delicacies."*

society. Let your business reach all levels of society including the kings! Let you have easy access to the luminaries and kings so that you may serve them in all respects!

10. **Neftali**[75]: May you be the blessing of the fruits of your womb, may you be the beauty of your offspring and pass it on. May you have the agility and ability to handle and endure hunger and thirst like the hinds; may you be the retreat for the protection of your offspring or the fruits of their womb! like a tree, may you bear beautiful branches (another version translated Neftali is a large tree that bears beautiful branches). May your words always be beautiful to hear!

11. **Joseph**[76]: May you be the offspring of a fertile

---

75. **Genesis 49: 21** *"Naphtali is a doe let loose that bears beautiful fawns."*

76. **Genesis 49: 22 - 26** *"Joseph is a fruitful bough, a fruitful bough by a spring; his branches run over the wall. The archers bitterly attacked him, shot at him, and harassed him severely, yet his bow remained unmoved; his arms were made agile by the hands of the Mighty One of Jacob (from there is the Shepherd, the Stone of Israel), by the God of your father who will help you, by the Almighty who will bless you with blessings of heaven above, blessings of the deep that crouches beneath, blessings of the breasts and of the womb. The blessings of your father are mighty beyond the blessings of my parents, up to the bounties of the everlasting hills. May they be on the head of Joseph, and on the brow of him who was set apart from his brothers."*

tree! May you grow near a spring of water, be fertile in growth or in expansion; may you bear much fruit because of your attachment to the spring! The productivity of fruit. May you go beyond the limits set, go beyond barriers; may you be able to defend yourself by using your bow against the arrows of your enemies, may your hands keep their suppleness thanks to the support of the Almighty of Jacob, the Shepherd, and the Rock. God's help is with you, and his blessing too. Thou art watered from heaven by rain and from earth by the springs of the earth; children and riches; may thou enjoy the better blessings of the earth, the ancient riches of the hills, standing out among his brethren!

12. **Benjamin**[77]: May you always succeed in your hunting, you win your battles, tear your enemies apart. You always hit your target and share the prey or the booty with others, you have liberality.

You understand that these words and promises are the greatest blessings that Jacob left to his children. Nowhere is there any reference to the material goods or wealth that he left to his children. The greatest legacy

---

77. **Genesis 49: 27** *"Benjamin is a ravenous wolf, in the morning devouring the prey and at evening dividing the spoil."*

you can leave to your children are the words and blessings you speak to them. These words are more powerful than wealth because they engender destiny with all the appropriate resources.

CONCLUSION

The word is God's mechanism and means of undertaking all things. This is one of his main activities; he calls on the man created in his image to proceed in the same way if he wants to have an impact in his works.

God's system of dominion proceeds through the stage of the word both at the beginning level and at the same time at the last finishing stage. When things are expressed, they are at the same time done because we believe that what we say happens based on the principle laid down by Jesus in the book of **Mark 11: 23-24**.

Thus, in the process of creation and mastery of things in God, time is not linear but rather punctual, the beginning and the end occur at the same time. When God thinks and speaks a thing, it has finished and begun at the same time. Thus, like God, we must match the moment of our belief with that of the quality of the declaration of our faith.

In the process of domination and mastery of things, the process of naming is very important. For everything God has created, He has given a name. This one has an identity with what is named or called. The name therefore has as much power as the message it carries. It contains a considerable spiritual and legal heritage; it gives rights and privileges to whoever uses and wears it.

In this way, the one who invokes, calls, and uses the name of Jesus benefits from his authority and his powers.

The spiritual world knows the power of the name because it also knows the power of the word.

Nature and creation are recipients of orders from God, and as he has given man his identity to continue acting as such, he can in turn command and dominate in many areas.

Thus, no thing or environment resists the voice of God, especially when it comes to a given order. The word is an instrument at man's disposal to command and give orders in his environment. God has given us the power to instruct situations, problems, and circumstances to execute.

Everything that God has created reacts to the word in the spiritual world, so mountains, nature, visible and invisible things respond to words because they have ears to listen to the word. God listens and hears man when he speaks to nature.

Words are the best way to bring invisible things to the visible world.

Prayer is also a plea; in this sense, it serves us much more to change the situations in which the enemy uses his weapon of accusation. He uses God's law against God's children when there is an obvious reason to accuse and condemn. Prayers (words) are a means of making arguments against the accusations and condemnations of the enemy. But we know that there is already a judgment that has been rendered, lifting any condemnation against those who are in Christ. It fell upon the Savior and Lord Jesus. Moreover, he has become our Lawyer before the just Judge. As such, he pleads his substitution on the cross, he has taken our place, he made himself sin, he has carried all our sicknesses, our curses, our poverty, better all condemnation and punishment have fallen on him and therefore God can no longer do anything against those who are in Christ. No accuser can succeed in a trial (a case) against the one who has faith in him.

Jesus-Christ is the best Lawyer who knows how to defend man because he knows him, because he has been himself, and he knows God because he himself is God.

Our lawyer prevents any condemnation against God's chosen people. No one can accuse them. He is also a lawyer-mediator before God to save us the price to pay; himself being the best price of the ransom.

The prophet Isaiah wants us to also be litigants before God so that we can make changes in decisions already made but against us. We need arguments as litigants. The argument of the pleading is important to bring God to change His judgments, rulings, and resolutions.

It is possible to win before God, but everything depends on the arguments we present before Him. His will is that there be a race of litigants to prevent his judgments in this world where there is everything necessary to stir up his anger, which can bring destruction. In our prayer-pleadings, the blood of the Lamb, the word of our testimony, the sacrifice of life for God are the best arguments to present as means.

In building his destiny, God endowed Christians with words in tongues as important materials. Words in tongues build your destiny and create new situations in your life. They are an encrypted means of communication to speak to one's life and God about the mysteries. Lyrics in language build and impact our destiny to the extent that they build it by what is really needed as needs, instruments, and tools.

So, we have a double advantage here, we communicate with God in encrypted language, and we know exactly how to conform to God's plans and thoughts in our prayer in tongues. Also, the Holy Spirit knows God's thoughts or plans; he helps us to pray according to it.

He who speaks in tongues prays more than he who

prays with understanding, he significantly improves his prayer life.

Those who speak in tongues also do a very beneficial work for their spiritual life, that of building himself up and strengthening himself. In both systems of spiritual edification, speaking in tongues is the best way to build one's destiny.

If simple words have the capacity to give life or death, how can they not be the words that are inspired by the Holy Spirit? For it is in spirit that we speak in tongues, we say things that only Spirit understands.

He who speaks in tongues builds his destiny with solid materials that are powerful words with direct and boomerang effects, back on his own life.

The words we speak also have effects on our offspring; we would have to be aware of this to affect them in the best way. Because words about your children or offspring are always true. And as Christians, we are also recipients of Abraham's blessing.

Today, you can accept Jesus-Christ as your personal savior and lord.

1. God loves you with unconditional love and does not condemn you, in addition to having a wonderful plan for your life.

"For God so loved the world, that he gave his only Son, that whoever believes in him should not perish but have eternal life." **John 3: 16**

"The thief comes only to steal and kill and destroy. I came that they may have life and have it abundantly." **John 10 : 10**

"For I know the plans I have for you, declares the Lord, plans for welfare and not for evil, to give you a future and a hope." **Jeremiah 29: 11**

2. You are a sinner, and you need God's salvation.

"For all have sinned and fall short of the glory of God." **Romans 3: 23**

"For the wages of sin is death, but the free gift of God is eternal life in Christ Jesus our Lord." **Romans 6: 23**

3. There is no salvation in anyone else but Jesus Christ. He is God's only solution.

"And there is salvation in no one else, for there is no other

name under heaven given among men by which we must be saved." **Acts 4: 12**

"Jesus said to him, "I am the way, and the truth, and the life. No one comes to the father except through me." **John 14: 6**

4. Your decision to receive Him by faith as your Savior and Lord is crucial.

"For by grace you have been saved through faith. And this is not your own doing; it is the gift of God, 9not a result of works, so that no one may boast." **Ephesians 2: 8-9**

"Because, if you confess with your mouth that Jesus is Lord and believe in your heart that God raised him from the dead, you will be saved. For with the heart, one believes and is justified, and with the mouth one confesses and is saved. For the Scripture says, "Everyone who believes in him will not be put to shame." **Romans 10: 9 -11**

Prayer

Lord, thank you for your love and plan for my life. I acknowledge that I am a sinner and deprived of your glory, and death awaits me. I believe that you died for my sins, and I accept and receive you as my Savior and Lord. I believe and confess you as my Savior and Lord. Thank you for the forgiveness of sins and the eternal life you give me.

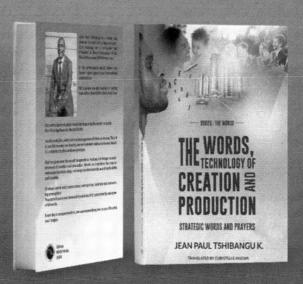

Our entire destiny is determined and shaped by the words we speak.

Our life is significantly affected by the words we declare, which are the consequences of what we believe. Thus, it is possible to make our destiny, our environment and our universe beautiful and better by the words we proclaim.

God has given man the mouth to operate as he does, the tongue as an instrument of creation and production. Words are therefore the creation and production technology, to change and dominate the world, both visible and invisible.

Strategic words and prayers create your spiritual environment and working atmosphere.

You can influence and command the land on which you stand by your powerful words.

Every day is an opportunity to announce something new in your life using your tongue.

get yours amazon kindle   Bow Movement

www.bowmovement.org

Copyright © 2024 **Jean Paul Tshibangu**

MASTERING AND BUILDING THROUGH WORDS.

THE ART OF AFFECTING ONE'S DESTINY.

All Rights Reserved.

This book or any portion thereof may not be reproduced or used in any manner whatsoever without the express written permission of the publisher except for the use of brief quotations in the book review.

BOW Media, Atlanta, 2024

Printed in United States of America.
For more information, or to book an event, contact:
http://www.bowmovement.org

Made in the USA
Columbia, SC
03 August 2024

69cbede7-8515-4271-ab3a-fca26a27d173R01